GENERAL EDITOR: JAMES GIBSON

JANE AUSTEN	*Emma* Norman Page
	Sense and Sensibility Judy Simons
	Persuasion Judy Simons
	Pride and Prejudice Raymond Wilson
	Mansfield Park Richard Wirdnam
SAMUEL BECKETT	*Waiting for Godot* Jennifer Birkett
WILLIAM BLAKE	*Songs of Innocence and Songs of Experience* Alan Tomlinson
ROBERT BOLT	*A Man for All Seasons* Leonard Smith
CHARLOTTE BRONTË	*Jane Eyre* Robert Miles
EMILY BRONTË	*Wuthering Heights* Hilda D. Spear
JOHN BUNYAN	*The Pilgrim's Progress* Beatrice Batson
GEOFFREY CHAUCER	*The Miller's Tale* Michael Alexander
	The Pardoner's Tale Geoffrey Lester
	The Wife of Bath's Tale Nicholas Marsh
	The Knight's Tale Anne Samson
	The Prologue to the Canterbury Tales Nigel Thomas and Richard Swan
JOSEPH CONRAD	*The Secret Agent* Andrew Mayne
CHARLES DICKENS	*Bleak House* Dennis Butts
	Great Expectations Dennis Butts
	Hard Times Norman Page
GEORGE ELIOT	*Middlemarch* Graham Handley
	Silas Marner Graham Handley
	The Mill on the Floss Helen Wheeler
T. S. ELIOT	*Selected Poems* Andrew Swarbrick
HENRY FIELDING	*Joseph Andrews* Trevor Johnson
E. M. FORSTER	*A Passage to India* Hilda D. Spear
	Howards End Ian Milligan
WILLIAM GOLDING	*The Spire* Rosemary Sumner
	Lord of the Flies Raymond Wilson
OLIVER GOLDSMITH	*She Stoops to Conquer* Paul Ranger
THOMAS HARDY	*The Mayor of Casterbridge* Ray Evans
	Tess of the d'Urbervilles James Gibson
	Far from the Madding Crowd Colin Temblett-Wood
BEN JONSON	*Volpone* Michael Stout
JOHN KEATS	*Selected Poems* John Garrett
RUDYARD KIPLING	*Kim* Leonée Ormond
PHILIP LARKIN	*The Whitsun Weddings* and *The Less Deceived* Andrew Swarbrick
D.H. LAWRENCE	*Sons and Lovers* R. P. Draper

MACMILLAN MASTER GUIDES

MACMILLAN MASTER GUIDES

THE CHANGELING

BY THOMAS MIDDLETON AND

WILLIAM ROWLEY

TONY BROMHAM

MACMILLAN

First published 1986 by
MACMILLAN PRESS LTD
Houndmills, Basingstoke, Hampshire RG21 6XS
and London
Companies and representatives
throughout the world

ISBN 0–333–40731–8

A catalogue record for this book is available
from the British Library.

11 10   9   8   7   6   5   4
05   04   03   02   01   00   99   98

Printed in Malaysia

CONTENTS

GENERAL EDITOR'S PREFACE

The aim of the Macmillan Master Guides is to help you to appreciate the book you are studying by providing information about it and by suggesting ways of reading and thinking about it which will lead to a fuller understanding. The section on the writer's life and background has been designed to illustrate those aspects of the writer's life which have influenced the work, and to place it in its personal and literary context. The summaries and critical commentary are of special importance in that each brief summary of the action is followed by an examination of the significant critical points. The space which might have been given to repetitive explanatory notes has been devoted to a detailed analysis of the kind of passage which might confront you in an examination. Literary criticism is concerned with both the broader aspects of the work being studied and with its detail. The ideas which meet us in reading a great work of literature, and their relevance to us today, are an essential part of our study, and our Guides look at the thought of their subject in some detail. But just as essential is the craft with which the writer has constructed his work of art, and this may be considered under several technical headings – characterisation, language, style and stagecraft, for example.

The authors of these Guides are all teachers and writers of wide experience, and they have chosen to write about books they admire and know well in the belief that they can communicate their admiration to you. But you yourself must read and know intimately the book you are studying. No one can do that for you. You should see this book as a lamp-post. Use it to shed light, not to lean against. If you know your text and know what it is saying about life, and how it says it, then you will enjoy it, and there is no better way of passing an examination in literature.

JAMES GIBSON

ACKNOWLEDGEMENTS

Especial thanks to Alfred and Marthe Martin in the tranquillity of whose house in the Auvergne a substantial part of this book was written.

NOTE: References to the play use the act, scene and line numbering of the New Mermaid edition, ed. Patricia Thomson (Ernest Benn, 1964).

Cover illustration: the painting *Two Lovers* by Bordoni.

Every effort has been made to trace all the copyright holders but if any have been inadvertently overlooked the publishers will be pleased to make the necessary arrangement at the first opportunity.

1 LIFE AND BACKGROUND

1.1 THOMAS MIDDLETON (1580–1627)

Thomas Middleton was born in London in 1580, the son of a 'citizen and bricklayer' who died when the dramatist was 5 years old. His mother, Anne, soon married again, but the marriage was not a happy one, and Thomas Middleton grew up in a turbulent atmosphere of family quarrels and lawsuits. His father had had property interests and died leaving Anne Middleton a well-to-do city widow, but she had to protect the family legacy from her grasping second husband. Perhaps because the many lawsuits had drained the family finances, Thomas, who went up to Queen's College, Oxford, in 1598, did not complete his degree. His writing career began at this time with the publication of poems and pamphlets, but before long, in 1601, we hear of him in London where he is said to be 'accompaninge the players'. It is not clear whether by this is meant that he had actually attached himself to a group of actors, but clearly an interest in, and connection with, the theatre is indicated. It is not surprising, therefore, that within a year or two the records indicate that he was writing for the stage and that his career as a dramatist had begun.

The exact dates of writing of many of his plays are uncertain, but we know that in his early years he wrote largely satirical comedies of contemporary London life, such as *A Mad World, My Masters* (?1604), *Michaelmas Term* (?1605), *A Trick to Catch the Old One* (?1606) and *A Chaste Maid in Cheapside* (?1612). These plays present the city as a place where almost everyone is in pursuit of money or sex, or both. The most successful characters are those who are most cunning and inventive in their attempts to outwit others in order to acquire what they want. Often in these plays the audience experiences a sense of tension between enjoyment of the antics of the tricksters and con-men, and the moral viewpoint which is also present. By about 1613, Middleton almost entirely ceased to write satiric comedies of this kind, and in the middle part of his career he wrote a number of tragicomedies, such as *The Witch* (1614) and *A Fair Quarrel* (1617), which do not appear to have been very successful. His greatest theatrical successes were to come in the 1620s, when he turned to tragedy in *Women Beware Women* (?1621) and *The Changeling* (1622), and to political satire in *A Game at Chess* (1624).

The tragedies do not mark a sudden change in Middleton's work. Although they were written ten or more years later, they show development of themes, attitudes and techniques found in the earlier city comedies. You may be surprised to find that in *The Changeling* there is not only a comic sub-plot, but there are also comic elements in the main plot.

Middleton ended his career as a dramatist with the political satire, *A Game at Chess*, which ran for nine consecutive days, a most unusual phenomenon in the theatre of the time as it was usual for a different play to be presented each day. The play drew large audiences and finally had to be withdrawn because of official disapproval. Some members of the company were imprisoned and Middleton had to go into hiding. He died in 1627.

1.2 WILLIAM ROWLEY (?1585–?1625)

Much less is known about Middleton's collaborator on *The Changeling*, William Rowley. The exact dates of his birth and death are uncertain, but we know that he was an actor who specialised in comic roles. He collaborated with Middleton on a number of plays from about 1615 onwards, often writing the comic scenes and possibly playing the main comic parts. In *The Changeling* it is generally believed that he was responsible for the comic sub-plot and for the opening and closing scenes of the play. Rowley wrote many plays of his own, such as *All's Lost by Lust* (?1619) and *The Birth of Merlin* (?1619), but they are rarely if ever performed today and he is chiefly known for his collaborative work with more accomplished dramatists such as Middleton.

1.3 A NOTE ON COLLABORATION

Although we are not particularly accustomed today to dramatists writing plays together for the theatre, collaboration of writers of television scripts is quite common. Collaboration was not unusual in the Elizabethan and Jacobean theatre. Both Middleton and Rowley wrote plays with other dramatists during their careers. Plays of the period often have more than one plot (or line of action) and so it was possible for separate parts of the work to be written by different people. Probably before the writing commenced there would have been a joint planning stage when the dramatists would have discussed together the plotting and arrangement of scenes. At this stage the connections between the plots and the ways in which those connections were to be made would have been worked out. Although the two plots of *The Changeling* were mainly written by different people and seem at first reading to be very separate and distinctive in style, closer study will show that there are important connections between them which reveal that they are part of a unified design (see Section 4.5).

1.4 ELIZABETHAN AND JACOBEAN DRAMA

Historically, the term 'Elizabethan' refers to the reign of Elizabeth I (1558–1603) and 'Jacobean' to the reign of her successor, James I (1603–25). However, the terms are sometimes used rather more loosely when applied to the drama of the period. Dramatists do not suddenly start to write different kinds of plays simply because a new monarch comes to the throne, but changing social, political, religious and theatrical conditions are likely to bring about changes in literature and drama. There is a noticeable change at about the turn of the century. When applied to the drama, the distinguishing labels 'Elizabethan' and 'Jacobean' do not so much indicate precisely whether a play was written before or after 1603, but denote the contrasting characteristics and moods which are to be found in the earlier and later literature of the period 1558–1625.

The reasons for the change in the mood of the times reflected in the drama are many and complex, and it is certainly not possible to explain here, except in the simplest of terms, matters about which historians are not in complete agreement. Elizabeth I had been a charismatic ruler, who knew how to inspire the loyalty and devotion of her subjects, thus providing a focus for national unity. She was celebrated, indeed almost deified, as the Virgin Queen, Gloriana, or Astraea, in art, poetry and music. In 1588 England achieved a significant victory over its long-standing enemy, Spain, with the defeat of the Armada, an event which bolstered national pride and established a mood of optimism. Under the already-long reign of Elizabeth, the country seemed to have achieved a degree of security and stability in marked contrast to the reigns of her two immediate predecesors. She established a civilised and cultured court of men like Sir Philip Sidney and Sir Walter Raleigh who were as accomplished poets and writers as they were men of action. But Elizabeth reigned for forty-five years, and in the latter part of her reign many of her subjects would have known no other ruler but her. The ageing of the queen and the inevitability of her approaching death at the turn of the century must have focused their minds upon the facts of time, change and mortality, and generated feelings of insecurity and uncertainty, which were increased by Elizabeth's refusal until the last moment to name her successor. The uncertainty of the succession raised the possibility of civil war and instability when the queen died. Though the peaceful succession of James I may have calmed immediate fears, the new king lacked the charismatic appeal of his predecessor and her ability to inspire loyalty and devotion. Conflicts and divisions of a religious, political and social nature which had existed before he came to the throne now became more apparent and pronounced. They were increased by growing economic problems and by social changes associated amongst other things with the development of mining and industrial enterprises. James adopted a policy of peace with Spain which was abhorrent to many patriotically-minded Englishmen who had always regarded the Spanish as their enemies. In 1619 the King executed Sir Walter Raleigh, a figure associated with the days of Elizabeth when England was at war with Spain. Tensions between the King and Parliament led to questioning and debate about the nature of the state and of sovereign authority. A mood of critical questioning was abroad. In contrast to the court of Elizabeth, the court of James came to be associated in popular opinion with corruption and wanton extravagance. All these factors contributed to the mood of disillusion, which was further increased in 1612 by the death of Prince Henry, the heir to the throne, who people had hoped would bring a better and more glorious future. The mood denoted by the term 'Jacobean', then, is a mood of pessimism, scepticism, disillusion and uncertainty, arising from a powerful awareness of time, change and human mortality, in direct contrast to the mood we have called 'Elizabethan', which is characterised by optimism and assurance, delight in life, and a belief in the possibilities of human achievement.

In the drama at the turn of the century there are noticeable changes in tone and in the kinds of play which were written. Satiric and realistic comedy became predominant. You have only to compare Thomas Dekker's genial and idealistic comedy, *The Shoemaker's Holiday* (1599), which is set in London, with some of the city comedies of Ben Jonson or Thomas Middleton written only a few years later, which also have London settings, to see the kinds of change which occur. Dekker has an optimistic view of human nature as essentially good, and in his play he presents a society which is unified through the operation of human love, benevolence and concern for others. At the end of the play, Simon Eyre, the shoemaker who has become Lord Mayor, holds a banquet at which all ranks of society are present, from the King down to the young London apprentices, a scene expressive of social harmony. In Middleton's London comedies we are shown a very different society, in which people pursue their own ends regardless of others, using deception and underhand means to achieve their desires. The supposedly respectable and responsible members of society such as magistrates and city merchants, are shown as little better than the common rogues and con-men that society condemns. Human nature in these plays is regarded as essentially corrupt.

Broadly speaking, in the sphere of tragedy, in the plays of John Webster, George Chapman, Cyril Tourneur and Thomas Middleton for instance, we can note a similar change of tone and mood from Elizabethan to Jacobean. Elizabethan tragedies tend to present a fairly clear system of values; man and his world are essentially good and the destructive force of evil is an aberration usually concentrated in a single character who is finally overcome by the forces of good, with a subsequent restoration of order and harmony. Character-drawing is usually fairly simple, with types rather than individuals being presented. Characters may display single major characteristics such as purity, greed, or foolishness. Jacobean tragedies are darker in mood and more questioning in spirit. They are often ambiguous; it is not always easy to divide characters into the simple categories of good and evil. Character-drawing becomes more complex as attempts are made to portray individuals rather than types. With the exception of *Hamlet* (1601) all Shakespeare's great tragedies were written in the historical Jacobean period, and display an interest in understanding why individual characters behave as they do. Middleton, too, in *The Changeling* is obviously interested in exploring the 'psychology' of Beatrice-Joanna, an adolescent girl who is just discovering what power her sexual attractiveness gives her. The sense of the complexity and individuality of human beings which we find in the work of Shakespeare and his greatest Jacobean contemporaries leads also to a consideration of the difficulties of knowing the true nature of another person. Alsemero's cry of anguish in the last scene of *The Changeling*, 'oh, cunning devils!/ How should blind men know you from fair-fac'd saints?' (V, iii, 108–9) expresses what is a major concern not only of this play but also of others in this period. The audience has known all along, as he has not, the true nature of Beatrice, through Middleton's use of soliloquy and asides (see Section 4.4). In John Webster's tragedy, *The White Devil* (1612), the audience is made to appreciate the problem through its own experience of the central character, Vittoria Corombona. She is shown in varying contexts and emotional situations, but Webster does not reveal, as Middleton does with Beatrice, what she is thinking, so that we are never quite sure to what extent Vittoria is a corrupt and scheming woman and to what extent she is wronged and defamed. The very title of the play, *The White Devil* is ambiguous and draws our attention to the problem of understanding the truth of a person. White is associated with goodness and purity, and is therefore the opposite of what we would expect of a devil, but is the phrase 'white devil' meant to indicate a creature who is really evil (that is, devil) but who appears to be good (white), or exactly the opposite, one who appears to be evil but is in reality pure?

Although the presentations of Vittoria and Beatrice are different, both Webster and Middleton, like other Jacobean dramatists, are concerned with problems of knowing and perceiving truth. Both also have in common a sense of a world pervaded by corruption. In the court worlds of Webster's tragedies, *The White Devil* (1612) and *The Duchess of Malfi* (1613–14), everyone is tainted by the corruption that surrounds them. In *The Changeling* the corruption is located within the characters themselves. Middleton presents a pessimistic view of human nature, flawed by original sin (see Section 3.3), the result of which is that man carries within him the seeds of his own destruction through a natural tendency to sin. The prison and the cage are recurring images in Webster's tragedies: his characters are trapped within their decadent court worlds, whilst Middleton's cannot escape from themselves and the fact of their sinful nature.

Whereas in Elizabethan writers there is a sense of human possibilities for development through love, courage, nobility, the exercise of virtue, or the appreciation of beauty, Jacobean writers have an overwhelming sense of human limitations, of man as a physical creature subject to disease, the effects of time, and death, whose achievements are illusory or merely transitory, and who seems incapable of perceiving truth or achieving harmony and fulfilment. Shakespeare's work spans both the Elizabethan and Jacobean periods and reflects the changes of mood. In *Hamlet* (1601), a play which by date is strictly Elizabethan but by mood is Jacobean, the central character has a speech which reflects the change. Hamlet describes what a magnificent creature man is but ends with the thought that he is subject to death; he is 'this quintessence of dust', Adam created by God from the dust and returning to it in death. It is this thought of man's mortality which seems to call in question the value of the living person and his wondrous faculties:

What a piece of work is man, how noble in reason, how infinite in faculties, in form and moving how express and admirable, in action how like an angel, in apprehension how like a god: the beauty of the world, the paragon of animals - and yet, to me, what is this quintessence of dust?

(William Shakespeare, *Hamlet*, II, ii, 303-8)

The Jacobean mood and the preoccupation with death is epitomised in *The Revenger's Tragedy* (1605-6) a play usually ascribed to Cyril Tourneur, but which several scholars think was written by Thomas Middleton. In the central scene, Vindice dresses up the skull of his dead mistress, Gloriana, and anoints the lips with poison, in a plot to kill the lecherous duke who had caused her death. The duke comes to the darkened summer house thinking that he is to meet a court lady whom he will seduce. In the shadows he mistakes the disguised skull for the living woman, kisses it, and dies an agonising death. This sensational scene presents a powerful image of the reality of human mortality which destroys physical beauty and brings to an end those human passions that seemed so important. It is a scene full of ironies, not the least of which is that the Duke, in pursuing his lustful pleasures brings about his death. It is also a scene which combines horror and grim humour, an effect which is characteristic of Jacobean tragedy. You will find in the list of Further Reading a book by Nicholas Brooke which examines Jacobean dramatists' use of this combination of elements in their plays.

The Changeling is by date a Jacobean play; in mood it is also unequivocally Jacobean. Its central concern with change and the process of human corruption, with its emphasis upon sex; the probing and questioning nature of its analysis of human character and action; the dramatist's ironic vision, and his technique of presenting scenes of sensational horror and evoking grim laughter at the same time; all these features make *The Changeling* a characteristic play of its period.

1.5 REVENGE PLAYS

Although we can trace changes in the kinds of plays which were written in the Elizabethan and Jacobean periods, we can also see some continuity in the sphere of tragedy where the pursuit of revenge was the most fre-quently-treated subject in plays stretching from the 1580s well into the seventeenth century. This subject for tragedy is a very ancient one. In the *Oresteia*, by the Greek dramatist Aeschylus (525–456 BC), Orestes, the son of King Agamemnon, has to avenge the murder of his father, but the crime has been committed by his mother, and so, in following the moral imperative to avenge his father, Orestes transgresses another divine law forbidding matricide and has to suffer for it.

The ancient tragic writer who had most influence on the Elizabethans was the Roman dramatist, Seneca (died 65 AD), ten of whose tragedies were published in translation in 1581. The plays were characterised by violence and bloodshed. Thomas Kyd's *The Spanish Tragedy* (1592), influenced by Seneca, was very popular and established a formula which was used by other dramatists in the period. At the beginning of the play a ghost appears calling for vengeance on those who killed him. In the play, Horatio is murdered. His father, Hieronimo, has to find out the identity of the murderers, and then appeals to the king for justice. Failing to obtain it by legal means, he decides to seek revenge himself. He and his wife become mad. Eventually he kills his enemies and dies himself. The appearance of the ghost, the need to discover the identities of the murderers, and the planning of the means to destroy them, were all features which were repeated in subsequent revenge plays, as were scenes of violence and bloodshed, and often madness. Shakespeare's *Titus Andronicus* (1594) was an early example of the genre, and *Hamlet* (1601) was perhaps its finest achievement. In *The Changeling* (1622) we find features of the revenge play: the ghost of Alonzo appears though it does not call for revenge; Tomazo is a revenger figure who tries to discover the murderer of his brother; madness is an important theme. However, much has changed from the early revenge plays. Tomazo is by no means the central character; he makes few appearances and the pursuit of revenge comes late in the play; when he does appear he is ineffectual, and, in fact, he does not exact his revenge nor does he die in the act like Hieronimo or Hamlet. The theme of madness is not directly connected with the revenge element, although at one point (V, ii) Tomazo begins to show signs of disturbed and irrational behaviour.

The changes from the earlier revenge-pattern reflect that Middleton and Rowley's concerns are with other matters, but they also indicate changes in the tradition of revenge plays over a period of about thirty years. In early plays like *The Spanish Tragedy* or *Hamlet*, the revenger, who is the central character, was an innocent person upon whom was imposed the task of achieving justice which could not be gained by legal methods. These revengers are corrupted and destroyed by that task. Later revenge plays, such as John Webster's *The White Devil* (1612) and *The Duchess of Malfi* (1614), present revengers who are not innocent but villainous, and often in later plays the reason for revenge is nothing as serious as murder but may be slighted honour, insults or jealousy. Revenge remains central to the structures of these plays as it is not in *The Changeling*. In Cyril Tourneur's *The Atheist's Tragedy* (1611), the clear message is that vengeance should be left to God, but it was not really until the 1620s that direct disapproval of revenge as a course of action was expressed very widely in the drama. Massinger's *The Fatal Dowry* (1619) presents such a direct criticism and, during this period William Rowley, Thomas Middleton, Philip Massinger, John Ford and Sir William D'Avenant in particular treat revenge as futile and mistaken.

In *The Changeling* Tomazo is presented as slightly ridiculous and ineffectual when he tries to discover who has murdered his brother. This is Middleton and Rowley's way of showing that the revenger is not needed since evil brings about its own destruction and truth will come to light. The story on which the main plot is based appeared in a collection which showed the working of divine vengeance in the punishment of murderers. In *The Changeling*, if it is not exactly the hand of God which strikes down the evil-doors, there is implied a principle in the nature of things which ensures that evil does not ultimately survive. The concentration of the dramatists on the characters of Beatrice and De Flores rather than on Tomazo shows that it is the nature of evil, and matters of sin and retribution, which interest Middleton and Rowley.

1.6 SOURCES

Middleton and Rowley found the story for the main plot of *The Changeling* in a book by John Reynolds entitled *The Triumphs of God's Revenge against the Crying and Execrable Sin of Wilful and Premeditated Murder* (1621) and a translation by Leonard Digges of a Spanish story called *Gerardo The Unfortunate Spaniard* (1622). No definite source for the sub-plot has been identified. It is interesting to note the ways in which the dramatists used and changed their source material because these give us indications of their purpose and chief concerns in writing the play.

In Reynolds's book De Flores is simply a 'gallant young Gentleman', with no disfigurement or repulsive features. He kills Alonzo for Beatrice so that she may marry Alsemero, but he does not demand that she becomes his mistress. That only happens later when Beatrice falls out of love with Alsemero who suddenly and inexplicably develops an unwarranted jealousy. Alsemero then traps Beatrice and De Flores in the act of adultery and kills them. In the last part of the story, Tomazo, Alonzo's brother, challenges Alsemero to a duel and is killed by him in an underhand manner. Alsemero is then captured and executed. The substitution of Diaphanta for Beatrice on the wedding-night does not occur in Reynolds's story but is to be found in the other source.

One of the main differences between the play and its sources is the character of De Flores. He is a much more complex and interesting character than in Reynolds's story, where he makes no demands on Beatrice as reward for doing the murder. In Digges's story, however, a trusted servant who has fallen passionately in love with Isadaura (who corresponds to Beatrice) comes to her bedroom just before she is to be married. He confesses his love for her and threatens to kill her if she does not give in to him. He ravishes her and then Isadaura kills him while he is sleeping. Middleton combines the De Flores figure in Reynolds's story who kills Alonzo with the servant who threatens and ravishes Isadaura in the Digges source, but he adds much more to the character in the play. Middleton makes him a person who is repulsive in appearance, at first a victim of uncontrollable desires which force him to torture himself with sight of Beatrice, but who eventually, through knowing her secret, gains power over her. Particularly interesting is the way in which in the early part of the play Beatrice responds to him with fear as if he represents some danger to her. The relationship between Beatrice and De Flores is explored in depth and is made psychologically convincing in a way that is completely absent from the sources. One of the means by which Middleton achieves this is through the revelation of characters' feelings and thoughts in asides and soliloquies. The dramatists are obviously interested in exploring character and motivation. In Reynolds's story Alsemero becomes jealous for no reason, not because of something which has happened to rouse his suspicions. Nor is it clear why Alsemero does not avoid the duel with Tomazo when he only had to explain that it was Beatrice and De Flores who had killed Alonzo.

The dramatists also improve on Reynolds by creating continuity of effect and narrative. They show how one thing leads to another in a chain of causes and effects. Beatrice's desire for Alsemero leads her to use De Flores to rid herself of Alonzo; in doing so she puts herself into his power and is forced to become his mistress; this leads her to fear sleeping with Alsemero on their wedding-night lest he discovers she is not a virgin, so she arranges for Diaphanta to act as a substitute; this leads to Diaphanta's death. Beatrice goes deeper and deeper into sin. The main tragic effect of the play comes through watching Beatrice bring about her own destruction by starting a chain of consequences which she is unable to stop or reverse. Once she has embarked on this course of action there is an inevitability about the outcome. Beatrice may not be an attractive, virtuous or noble character, but it is terrible to watch her destroy herself and to sense her helplessness. It is this which gives the play such power and it is entirely the result of the dramatists' transformation of their sources.

2 SUMMARY AND CRITICAL COMMENTARY

Act I, Scene i

Summary

Alsemero has fallen in love with a woman he has seen in church. He decides to delay his departure from Alicante, much to the surprise of his friend, Jasperino, who cannot believe his eyes when Alsemero meets the woman, Beatrice-Joanna, and, uncharacteristically, kisses her and declares his love for her. Beatrice regrets that Alsemero has appeared only five days after she has agreed to marry Alonzo de Piracquo, at her father, Vermandero's, bidding. Jasperino starts to woo Diaphanta, Beatrice's waiting-woman. When De Flores, an ugly gentleman, comes to announce her father's arrival, Beatrice treats him harshly and expresses her loathing for him. Vermandero invites Alsemero to stay in his castle. He also insists that Beatrice should be married within a week to Alonzo. On hearing that Beatrice is already engaged, Alsemero desires to leave but is prevailed upon to stay. As she goes Beatrice drops a glove. When De Flores picks it up, she angrily throws down the other, refusing to wear anything touched by him. Left alone, De Flores expresses his infatuation for her.

Commentary

The situation is established with remarkable economy; the opening speech provides the information that Alsemero has fallen in love with a woman he has seen in church; Jasperino's reactions indicate that his friend's behaviour is most uncharacteristic; when they meet, the relationship between Beatrice and Alsemero is quickly established, as, later, is the fact that he is the son of an old friend of her father and therefore a welcome guest in the castle.

   Alsemero is the first of the changelings in the play. Until this moment he seems to have been a restless traveller, never staying anywhere for long. He has also never had a love relationship with a woman, despite the encouragement of his mother and friends, and his kissing Beatrice on their first meeting is a change of behaviour that Jasperino can hardly credit. Love has transformed his perception of things and he refuses to see them as others see them. The image of the weather-vane turning 'full in my face' (20), which would indicate on a literal level that the wind was adverse, has a hint of the ominous about it, and indeed the first sixty lines of the play contain a number of references to omens and premonitions which hint at impending evil. Alsemero assures Jasperino that he is well but then adds 'Unless there be some hidden malady/Within me, that I understand not' (23-4). The second servant is given a line containing an image of fire about to break out (51). Jasperino talks of Alsemero going backwards (46) and his insistence on the fact that if they are to travel to Malta this is the 'critical day' (50), suggesting that if they do not take this opportunity conditions are likely to prevent them, also carries a suggestion that this may be a critical and decisive day in other ways for Alsemero. The tragedy depends upon making decisions and committing a deed which cannot be reversed, and it focuses upon these critical moments or turning-points in the lives of Beatrice and Alsemero. The word 'omen' is used in the second line of the play, and there is a slightly strained feeling about the whole of Alsemero's opening speech. It begins with a question which he goes on to answer, but he seems to need to convince himself that his love for Beatrice is right. His argument that his intentions are virtuous and therefore not at odds with religion might be seen as special pleading since the church ('temple') should be the place for the worship of God and concentration on the spiritual life not for the worship of woman and concentration on physical beauty. The further argument that marriage is the means of restoring Man to perfection and recreating paradise (7-9) would certainly be seen to be dubious by anyone who believed Man's nature was flawed by the effects of Original Sin (see Section 3.3).

Beatrice's first dialogue with Alsemero has an element of flirtatiousness about it. She leads him on to declare his love for her first by not repelling his advances or even appearing surprised that he should kiss her, and then by engaging him in an apparently intellectual discussion as a scholar, asking about the nature of the love he professes as if love were one of the sciences (that is, areas of knowledge) and finally by going on to demand proof that it is true. She argues that the senses (in this case sight) and the reason ('judgment') should work together in the perception of truth, but that sometimes the eyes can deceive and 'tell us wonders/Of common things' (74-5). By saying this she encourages Alsemero to protest that his eyes have not deceived him about her and he responds with utmost assurance. The play thus begins with Alsemero declaring that he is able to perceive the truth about Beatrice's nature and that she is certainly no 'common thing' about which his eyes are telling him wonders. The development of the play will be towards his final acknowledgement of his blindness, his inability to perceive truth (V, iii, 108-9) and her acknowledgement that she is defiled and worthless, a common thing, and should be consigned to the sewer and oblivion (V, iii, 150-3). Alsemero argues here that his senses and reason (eyes and judgement) are in agreement about Beatrice and that there is nothing more to be done except for her to agree to their marriage. He behaves like the inexperienced man he is, thinking everything can be so neatly arranged without complication; he has fallen in love, he can prove that it is true love and that his beloved is a creature of worth, and the next logical step, therefore, is for them to marry. He seems to have little doubt that she will accept him, but her next speech (83-5) indicates that the situation is more complex than he sees it: her consent would depend upon her father. Then, in an aside which is in total contrast to the coolly-assured tone of her dialogue so far, there is a note of agitation and the suggestion that Alsemero has come too late for her to be able to consent, though the exact reason is not yet made clear to the audience. Her agitation is immediately increased by the entrance of De Flores.

The following part of the scene is contrasted with the previous part in a number of distinct ways. Beatrice's harsh and angry manner towards De Flores is set against her assured and courteous social manner towards Alsemero. Her response to De Flores here, and the even more violent nature of her reaction to him when he picks up her glove at the end of the scene (230), reveal a disturbingly unattractive aspect of this woman who at first seems so poised and charming. De Flores's aside (100-7) establishes that he is infatuated by her, though scorned, in contrast to Alsemero who is also smitten by Beatrice's appearance but who receives a more favourable reception. De Flores's experience of love is more complex than that of Alsemero who thinks that it is just a matter of finding true love and getting married: De Flores cannot stop finding opportunities to see Beatrice, and there is a suggestion that he will continue to do so to provoke her (105), as if he needs a strong emotional response from her, even if it be hatred rather than love. This idea is reinforced in the last speech of the scene. De Flores's statement that Beatrice cannot offer a reason for her dislike of him is borne out by her dialogue with Alsemero. The previous easy talk about eyes and judgement is shown up as artificial and unrelated to the realities of human experience. Beatrice's strong emotional response to the sight of De Flores cannot be explained rationally, and the use of words like 'infirmity' (109), 'frailty' (116), and 'imperfection' (118) suggest that such irrational feelings indicate some weakness of character. The speech of Alsemero (116-26) states that it is a weakness shared by mankind in general, with the implication that Man's ability to use his reason and to explain and govern his emotions is limited. The irrational dislike is described here as a poison (112, 127) and imagery of poison is to be found in the play as a whole, particularly associated with De Flores, who is described later as a poisonous snake (224). The sight of him is Beatrice's poison, as Alsemero's sight of her will prove his poison, although he does not know it. He does not answer Beatrice's question 'And what may be your poison, sir?' (127), perhaps indicating that he does not think that he has one.

The short dialogue between Jasperino and Diaphanta is not here simply to lighten the scene or to provide comic contrast, but is significant thematically. It contains references to sickness and the need for a cure (139-40) which connect with Jasperino's question about Alsemero's health and his comment about the hidden malady (22-4), and also with the references to poison and 'infirmity' (109) in the part of the scene which has just finished. Jasperino's sexual suggestions to Diaphanta that he could show her 'such a thing' (144) and his statement 'I'll discover no more now, another time I'll show thee all' (151-2) are linked in a bawdy and comic manner to the play's concern with secrets and with the revelation of hidden things. A few moments later, Vermandero is careful to establish Alsemero's credentials before showing him the secrets of the castle's defences. The castle will later hold the secret of the dead Alonzo deep in its inner recesses, and Beatrice will become fearful that her secret relationship with De Flores and her true nature will be discovered. The frequent use of asides in this scene and in the play as a whole underlines the fact that for much of the time the characters on stage do not know each other's inner thoughts or secrets. The dialogue between Jasperino and Diaphanta stands in direct contrast to the meeting of Alsemero and Beatrice. Jasperino is sexually suggestive and physical in his approach, whereas Alsemero's speeches lack direct reference to the physical reality of his attraction to Beatrice and are concerned with proving his love intellectually. Whereas Beatrice seems to lead Alsemero on to his declaration of love, Diaphanta fends off Jasperino's direct advances in an amused, though perhaps not entirely discouraging, manner.

Alsemero's hopes are raised and almost immediately dashed when Vermandero invites him to stay in the castle as a family friend but reveals that Beatrice is to marry Alonzo de Piracquo within a week. Imagery of poison recurs as Alsemero responds to his invitation to the wedding with the words 'He means to feast me, and poisons me beforehand' (207). This is an aside and it is noticeable how the number of asides increases as the scene draws to its close, revealing the real thoughts of the characters behind the social façade. One of the most important occurs at 155, where there is an indication that Beatrice will become a changeling, just as Alsemero was at the beginning of the scene. She will turn her affections to Alsemero and away from Alonzo. She has an experience of disorientation, of giddiness (156) just as Alsemero had at the opening when he admitted to Jasperino that he did not quite know where he was (22-3). The first scene presents these two people at the moment when both have experiences which disturb the pattern of their lives and which test their characters.

Vermandero is very insistent that Beatrice shall do as he wants. He dismisses in an insensitive way her protestations that she should not be so rushed to yield up her virginity and he also says that if Alonzo does not marry her 'I'll want/My will else' (219-20). The word 'will' is repeated several times in this scene, and is a term which appears to indicate 'a stubborn and reckless selfishness', as the editor, N. W. Bawcutt, puts it. Vermandero means that he is determined to have his way. Equally Beatrice is determined to have hers, as her response in an aside indicates (220), and at the end of the scene De Flores is just as determined to have his way, as the last line shows. The sexual suggestiveness of thrusting his fingers into Beatrice's gloves leaves no doubt what he wants. The situation of a serious clash of wills is forcefully established.

Act I, Scene ii

Summary

The scene changes to the madhouse kept by the doctor, Alibius, and his assistant, Lollio. The former is worried that while he is away on business his wife, Isabella, may be tempted to be unfaithful to him with the visitors who come to see the inmates of the madhouse. He instructs Lollio to watch her carefully and to ensure that she is not seen by the visitors. A gentleman, Pedro, brings a new patient, Antonio, to be admitted to the asylum. Lollio questions him to ascertain the extent of his mental deficiency. A noise of madmen is heard off-stage indicating that it is time for them to be fed.

Commentary

The audience experiences a change of mood from serious to comic as the action moves to the madhouse, but the second scene also establishes a basis for connections to be made between the main and sub-plots. The scene begins with a conversation about a secret. The word is repeated four times in the first seventeen lines. Alibius wants to keep his wife 'secret' not in the sense that the world shall not know of her existence, for as Lollio says ' 'tis too late to keep her secret' (8), but in the sense that no-one but himself shall have sexual relations with her. The madhouse, like Vermandero's castle, has secrets which must not be shown to, and therefore known by, strangers or enemies. Alibius uses the image of wearing his ring on his own finger (27) to suggest keeping his wife to himself, but it is an image which has a level of sexual suggestion, the more obvious to a Jacobean audience as 'finger' was sometimes used obscenely to signify 'penis'. The image of the ring and the finger will figure very significantly, with similar sexual symbolism, at the turning point of the main plot (III, iv) when De Flores presents Beatrice with Alonzo's ring on his severed finger. In the main plot, the other great secret besides the murder is a sexual one, that of Beatrice's relationship with De Flores.

The madhouse contains two different types of inmate, fools and madmen, and both Alibius and Lollio are, in jest, likened to them in the dialogue with Antonio (203), but Isabella is presented as neither foolish nor mad (65-6), the only sane and wise person in the place. The madhouse is presented in two ways which are of significance to the concerns of the play. It is first likened to a hospital where 'brainsick patients' (54) come to be cured by the doctor, Alibius (49-50). It is also presented as a school in which Lollio will teach the inmates and restore them to wisdom and sanity.

Alibius says to Lollio 'It will be long/ Ere all thy scholars learn this lesson' (79-80), and there are references to 'scholars' again at 228 and 237, and to 'schoolfellows' at 227. A major part of this scene is taken up with Lollio giving a lesson or examination to Antonio; he asks him questions to establish the state of his wits in order to decide in which form to place him (156-7). These features of the presentation of the madhouse which associate ideas of sickness needing to be cured and of foolishness needing to learn wisdom, reflect the main plot's concern with Man's moral sickness and his need to achieve moral wisdom.

The scene ends as the noise of madmen is heard within. Alibius says it is the time for them to be fed, and there is the suggestion that they are becoming restive rather like hungry animals. Indeed, Antonio's fear that the madmen may bite him associates them with animals of which one may need to take care. The noise of the unseen madmen may be intended to suggest that potentially dangerous forces are being held in check within the madhouse, with the possibility that there will be trouble if their appetites are not satisfied. Again this establishes a basis of connection with the main plot: imagery of food and feeding is associated there with sexual appetite and chaotic sexual desires will be shown in the main plot to lead characters to break moral constraints for the satisfaction of that appetite, with disastrous and destructive results. Unrestrained madness would be dangerous just as sexual desire unrestrained by morality is shown to be in the main plot.

Act II, Scene i

Summary

Beatrice gives Jasperino a message arranging a secret meeting with Alsemero. De Flores, whose infatuation seems to have intensified, comes to announce the arrival of Alonzo and is met with anger and harsh words from Beatrice, who is secretly terrified of De Flores. Vermandero, Alonzo and Alonzo's brother, Tomazo, arrive. Beatrice persuades her father to delay the wedding by three days, to which Alonzo agrees. Tomazo tries to persuade him to break off the match as he has noted Beatrice's coldness towards her future husband and he is convinced that she loves someone else. Alonzo refuses to heed the warning and expresses his belief in Beatrice's constancy and virtue.

Commentary

Beatrice, as a woman already engaged to be married, is doing something morally and socially questionable in secretly arranging a meeting with another man who has expressed ardent love for her, yet her words suggest nothing of the kind. She describes Jasperino's action in carrying the message to Alsemero as 'fair service' (1) as if he were performing some honourable errand of love, and her words 'Good angels and this conduct be your guide' (3) suggest that he is engaged on some mission to preserve virtue and goodness against the threat of evil, for which appropriately 'good angels' should be his protectors, rather than on arrangements for a clandestine meeting. Beatrice is clearly trying to transform the nature of the situation so that it is seen not as morally questionable but as unquestionably right. Her soliloquy which follows (6–26) confirms this impression and shows that it is not so much for Jasperino's benefit as for her own that she needs to present the situation in this way. Her speech, rather like that of Alsemero at the opening of the play, is an attempt to convince herself of the correctness of what she is doing. She uses the kind of argument based on the operation of judgement (reason) which Alsemero used to prove his love for her in the first scene. She argues that Alsemero is obviously a wise man because of his choice of friend to use as his messenger. However, her words are ironic since the audience knows from the earlier dialogue between Jasperino and Diaphanta that he is not particularly discreet, but a very down-to-earth character given to bawdy suggestion, and therefore more the kind of person suitable for sexual intrigue than for the refined conduct of love on a higher, more intellectual and spiritual plane, which is obviously how Beatrice wishes to see her relationship with Alsemero. Not only does she try to convince herself that he is a man of judgement and therefore more worthy than Alonzo of her love, but she also convinces herself that she too has judgement in being able to see that Alsemero is such a man. She now loves 'with the eyes of judgment' (13). All this is clearly rationalisation; she argues that what she wants to do is right by suggesting that it is sanctioned by her reason, the faculty which checks irrational desires, and enables Man to perceive truth and to follow the higher path of virtue. Her image of the worthy man sparkling like a diamond in the darkness (15–16) will have an ironic echo later in Act III, scene ii, when De Flores sees the diamond in the ring on Alonzo's finger sparkling in the darkness (III, ii, 20–2). In this scene Beatrice associates the diamond with Alsemero as the worthy man, whilst in the later scene the association is with Alonzo.

Our understanding of De Flores is enlarged in this scene. His first speech, an aside which reveals what he is thinking, refers to his infatuation for Beatrice as an ailment (27), an idea which is repeated later with the phrase 'mad qualm' (79); his passion is a sickness and a madness, an association we find in the sub-plot. It seems, too, that his sickness is becoming worse, indeed it is more like an addiction. He says that he has to see Beatrice, even though he suffers for it, with increasing frequency; 'Some twenty times a day' (29) is corrected, 'nay, not so little', almost as if the addiction is taking a stronger hold so that although he previously only needed to see her twenty times, he now needs to see her more often. At this point in the play De Flores is not a scheming villain but rather a victim of desires over which he has no control. The desires are irrational – he has 'small reason' (31) for them – and the image which he uses of himself of the bull being dragged again and again to the bull-baiting (80-1), a sport of the time in which bulls were set upon in a ring by dogs, emphatically presents him as victim. Like Alsemero and Beatrice, De Flores is in the grip of the powerful and irrational forces of love and desire, but, unlike them, he does not try to rationalise his feelings; he acknowledges irrationality as a human trait, and Man's consequent changeability gives him grounds for hope that eventually he may get what he wants. In speeches of rather sardonic humour he notes that much uglier men than he have been successful with beautiful women, and that it has been known for women who have been angry and antagonistic to end up in bed with the man they have attacked.

There is a clear sense of Beatrice and De Flores tormenting each other. He disturbs her by continually coming into her presence and she continually ill-treats and abuses him when he does. This torment is connected with the eyes: De Flores must see Beatrice with ever-increasing frequency (28, 78), and she cannot bear to see him (72-3). This scene makes clear, however, that there is more to Beatrice's repulsion than the ugliness of De Flores. He himself says that she reacts 'As if danger or ill luck hung in my looks' (36), and her asides and soliloquies show that she feels he is a threat to her. She says that not only is he 'ill fac'd' but that he is 'ominous' (53), disturbing her more than anything else, and, when he leaves, she expresses again the sense of a danger so extreme that it affects her long after he has gone. Despite this, at the appearance of her father and Alonzo she dismisses her anxieties over De Flores as small compared to the 'torment' she now faces in marrying a man she no longer wants as a husband. The play shows that she was right to fear De Flores, but she suppresses that intuition of danger and evil because ridding herself of Alonzo, and the pursuit of her desire for Alsemero, are much more important to her.

Alonzo and Tomazo are contrasted in the latter part of the scene. Tomazo observes that Beatrice is cold towards Alonzo: she does not welcome him and wants the marriage delayed. Although this is quite obvious, Alonzo refuses to see and interpret the situation as Tomazo presents it. It is expressed in terms of seeing; Tomazo says 'did you mark the dullness of her parting now?' (123) but Alonzo has noticed nothing. Beatrice's eyes provide her with a warning about De Flores though she is unable to bring her reason to bear to explain her repulsion. Tomazo's eyes also provide a warning but he uses his reason (judgement) to deduce why Beatrice behaves as she does. Alonzo is obviously so determined to have his will, like the other main characters, in this case to marry Beatrice, that he sees only what he wants to see. Love blinds him to the reality which Tomazo presents. With some exasperation Tomazo says that he is a fool to bother about warning his brother (125-6), but it is clear to the audience that it is Alonzo who is being foolish. Tomazo also presents the love of Alonzo as a madness (153), and thus the 'blind' lover is shown to have the characteristics of the inhabitants of the madhouse of the subplot who are fools and madmen.

Act II, Scene ii

Summary

The secret meeting of Beatrice and Alsemero takes place. She expresses
the wish that she should not have to obey the command of her father and
marry Alonzo. Alsemero proposes to challenge Alonzo to a duel but
Beatrice fears the consequences; either her lover will die or he will be
arrested or have to flee. She suddenly lights upon the idea of using De
Flores to rid herself of Alonzo, and brings the meeting to an abrupt end as
she becomes absorbed by the idea. De Flores has watched the meeting
between the lovers and realises that Beatrice is on the edge of succumbing
to temptation. He knows that once she has fallen there will be the chance
for him to seek satisfaction of his desires. Beatrice pretends to treat him
pleasantly even to the extent of touching his face, and De Flores cannot
believe this change of behaviour and his apparent good fortune. He wishes
there were some way he could serve Beatrice. After pretending reluctance
to tell him, she eventually asks him to kill Alonzo, thinking she will be
able to pay De Flores and provide the means for him to go abroad, thus
ridding herself of both her fiancé, and the man she so much loathes and
fears. It is clear that De Flores sees his reward as being sexual favours from
Beatrice. The opportunity to carry out Beatrice's command occurs almost
immediately as Alonzo meets De Flores and asks him to show him round
the castle.

Commentary

The meeting between Beatrice and Alsemero is conducted at first as if it
were some honourable love-tryst rather than the illicit meeting it really is.
Diaphanta calls it 'a just meeting' (2) and refers to Alsemero as a 'complete
gentleman' (3); he speaks of secrets, such as that of the meeting, entrusted
by ladies to their serving women, as 'Things of most precious trust' (7);
Beatrice draws a comparison between Alsemero's appearance and prayers
being answered (8-12), saying that he is more wished for than heavenly
grace. Alsemero fell in love whilst in church where he should have been
worshipping God, and here Beatrice says that she values Alsemero and his
love more than spiritual things. These points suggest that their love is a
substitute for religion. The speech presents the answer to the prayers as
making good the deficiencies – that is the moral improvement – of the
person, and the implication of the reference seems to be that the love of
Alsemero will improve Beatrice even more than the answer of her prayers
to God. In terms of the play's concern with the deception of the eyes, her
expression of joy at seeing Alsemero is significant – 'I have within mine
eye all my desires' (8). Valuing Alsemero more highly than heavenly grace
suggests a dangerous distortion of values on Beatrice's part. She is of course
expressing the intensity of her joy through exaggeration but the way in
which she chooses to express this gives us an insight into her mind. There

are any number of comparisons she could have made to show how much 'more sweet' Alsemero is, but the one which the dramatist puts into her mouth reveals that she will put personal desire above moral and spiritual welfare. It is an ominous comparison, and provides an insight into the character which develops as the scene progresses and Beatrice first contemplates and then plans the murder of Alonzo. It is not the only disturbing element present in the opening of this scene. Whilst fine sentiments are being expressed, there are also hints that the realities of the situation are rather different; Diaphanta will not praise Alsemero too much because there would be the danger that Beatrice would overhear and be jealous, 'I dare not be too busy with my praises,/Th'are dangerous things to deal with' (3-4); as Beatrice thinks of Alonzo the tone of the meeting is disturbed by mention of 'envy' (16), 'enemy' (17), hate (17), and finally 'poison' (18). Beatrice compares the kiss she gives Alsemero with that which she has to give Alonzo, and wishes the latter could be poisoned (16-18). These words are expressed with similar vehemence and contain similar feelings to those she had previously expressed towards De Flores, and, indeed, when poison is mentioned again in this scene (46), it links Alonzo with him: her fiancé is a poison of which she will rid herself by the use of another poison, De Flores. The audience have seen Alonzo in the previous scene, and although he is presented as a person blinded by love, there is certainly no suggestion that he is an unsuitable man either in terms of character or appearance to be her husband. So the vehemence of Beatrice's expression of hatred indicates the completely irrational nature of her feelings and her need to justify her change of affections. By making Alonzo sound like a monster she is forced to kiss, but whom she would like to kill with poison – and we notice that the idea of killing is already there if only at a subconscious level – she makes Alsemero seem so much more a worthy partner. Her wish that there were no such person as Alonzo and that she did not have to heed her father's command (19-20) shows that her vehemence springs from an overwhelming desire to break free from constraints to achieve the freedom to do exactly as she wants. Alsemero responds to her projection of loathsomeness onto Alonzo by playing the role of the chivalrous lover who must rid his lady of an evil and troublesome suitor. He will perform a 'good service' (21) for the lady, and when she asks what that service might be, he replies 'The honourablest piece' bout man, valour' (27); he will challenge Alonzo to a duel. Alsemero has been established in the first act as a man inexperienced in love; his proposed course of action might be the brave and honourable thing to do in love fiction, and also if Alonzo really were as Beatrice wishes to present him, but her following speech quickly undercuts Alsemero's fine sentiments by presenting the reality of the situation. Just as in the first scene Alsemero thought that because he was in love with her, marrying Beatrice would be easy, he here naively assumes that ridding her of Alonzo will present no problems. She points out that a duel would solve nothing, as it would result either in the death of Alsemero, or in his arrest or enforced exile.

Beatrice's words make Alsemero's attempt to act the courageous lover seem rather ridiculous. A few years before the play was written, laws had been passed to prevent duelling, and Middleton and Rowley had written *A Fair Quarrel* (1617), a play about the duelling code. So when Beatrice says that a consequence of the duel may be that Alsemero will run into trouble with the law, the attention of the audience is drawn to the fact that he places his love above consideration of legal constraints. The dramatist thus shows a dangerous situation in which two people regard personal desire as of utmost value, overriding moral, social and legal constraints on which the order of society depends.

The final expression of the realities of what they are discussing comes from Beatrice as she says 'Blood-guiltiness becomes a fouler visage' (40), a statement that their desire to rid themselves of Alonzo would involve crime and consequent guilt. It also underlines the fact that despite the talk of honour and valour, if Alsemero killed Alonzo in a duel it would be tantamount to murder. It is significant that immediately she has spoken these words, Beatrice ceases to speak aloud, and we only hear her thoughts in an aside. Not only has the mention of 'fouler visage' suggested De Flores to her and how she might use him, but in speaking these words she is aware that she is in danger of revealing more of that side of her nature which is glimpsed when she encounters De Flores, and less of the lady of high thoughts and virtues she wishes to appear to Alsemero. The way in which Beatrice stumbles upon the solution to her problem by chance through the use of a particular phrase, 'fouler visage', is much more psychologically convincing than if she had sat down to think out what she might do. The second reference to 'poison' in this scene (46) shows that her earlier subconscious desire to kill Alonzo (18) is now rising to consciousness as she realises how she might use De Flores. It is interesting to note that this particular incident was not in Middleton's source, and is therefore probably his invention, indicating his dramatic sense and his ability to present characters from the inside. Also convincing is the immediate movement away from direct dialogue into asides, as she wishes to hide her thoughts from Alsemero. She becomes so absorbed by her idea that she ceases even to pay attention to Alsemero who has to make two attempts to get her to speak to him. It is ironic that at this very moment when she is thinking of a way to draw closer to Alsemero she actually ceases to communicate with him, hatching a secret which she will keep from him. Patricia Thomson says that this moment in the play reveals their complete lack of knowledge of each other (New Mermaid edition, p. xv.) and this is indeed true. From the start Beatrice adopted a poised and charming social manner with Alsemero, whilst the first encounter with De Flores, and her asides in the first scene, indicated other forces at work beneath this social veneer. While she tries to appear to him gracious, intelligent and virtuous, he, as this scene shows, tries to act in the manner he thinks appropriate to the chivalrous lover. Each therefore attempts not only to project an idealised image of themselves, but also to convince themselves of the ideal nature of the other. Alsemero's words just before he leaves 'You teach wisdom, lady' (52) indicate his idealised view of Beatrice; he refers to her without familiarity as 'lady', suggesting the kind of distance between the lover and the beloved found in much Elizabethan love-poetry, in which the lady inspires and transforms the lover through her consummate virtue and wisdom. However, the words are ironic coming just at the moment when the audience knows Beatrice is about to embark on a course of the utmost folly and evil.

De Flores has watched the meeting and realises that Beatrice will not be able to maintain the relationship with Alsemero as well as with Alonzo without sinning, and if she does so, then he is more likely to be able to satisfy his desire for her. He presents a view of woman completely opposite from that which Alsemero holds. He cynically argues that it is woman's nature, once she has given in to temptation, to sin more and more frequently. He uses an arithmetical image to express the idea and the exaggerated nature of the image, which presents the woman as eventually becoming so promiscuous as to become the supplier of sex to a whole army, creates the effect of black humour which was evident in De Flores's speeches in the previous scene. His speech here seems to imply that the knowledge of Beatrice's secret will give him power over her which would enable him to relinquish his role of passive victim. His words are full of sexual sugestion – 'serv'd' (59), 'put in' (60), 'point' (61), 'mounts' (62). It is ironic that at this moment Beatrice too is thinking of having the power to manipulate others so that she may live as she wants, ridding herself not only of Alonzo but also of De Flores at the same time.

Just as Beatrice keeps her real thoughts hidden from Alsemero, so she hides her real feelings from De Flores, using the words 'Cannot I keep that secret?' (68). The sense of hidden things and of characters not really knowing each other is emphasised by the number of asides in this part of the scene. Earlier scenes have established just how violently Beatrice loathes De Flores, and those feelings are repeated here (66-7), associating him with death ('sepulchre'), so that we realise what it must cost her to go through the pretence of being pleasant to him, and, consequently, how overriding must be her desire for Alsemero, for if she could not bear to wear gloves which De Flores had touched, how much more abhorrent it must be for her actually to have physical contact with him when she touches his face (81). Instinctively she knows that the way to work upon him is to use the power which her physical attractiveness gives her, and, indeed, De Flores's asides (79, 81, 86-7, 90-1) show just how immediately successful she is. As she led Alsemero on to declare his love for her in the first scene, so she leads De Flores on in a very calculated manner. She begins by taking him by surprise with kind and complimentary words; she follows these up by actually touching his face and promising to prepare with her own hands a cure for his disfiguring rash; she then says that his features are those suitable for the kind of man who might be trusted with some demanding task; he immediately responds by expressing the wish to perform such a task for her; she further encourages him by calling him 'my De Flores' (98) and then pretends reluctance to tell him what she wants him to do for her, which only encourages him to demand more fervently to be told; she finally tests his resolve by suggesting that the task will be violent and dangerous, and, when she is sure of him, she utters her terrible command in two brief lines, 'Then take him to thy fury! . . .Alonzo de Piracquo' (133-4).

De Flores begins by being unable to understand Beatrice's change of attitude towards him and he is quite overcome by it. The effect is distinctly humorous as his expectations of being 'rail'd at' are not fulfilled and he is quite bemused. By line 90 he begins to recover from his amazement and to take a grasp of the situation, 'I was blest/To light upon this minute; I'll make use on't' (90-1). As he becomes more consciously in control, the humour continues but now on the level of parody of Beatrice's words, with sexual innuendos on 'manhood', 'service', and 'mounts' (94-7), on 'creation' (107) and 'act' (122). The word 'service' is used nine times in the whole scene (21, 26, 54, 93, 96, 117, 119, 129, 140) and is a word which links Alsemero and De Flores. With the former it is used of honourable deeds performed for a lady by a lover or devoted follower. With De Flores it still has this sense on the surface, but a level of secondary sexual meaning, already present earlier in the scene – 'I'm sure both /Cannot be serv'd unless she transgress' (58-9) begins to creep in here as he realises that the performance of the service Beatrice asks may lead to service of another kind. His early asides reveal amazement and uncomprehending sexual pleasure at her touch, but the way he later picks up her words and gives them coarse innuendos, and his ironic comments:

BEATRICE   Thy reward shall be precious.
DE FLORES   That I have thought on;
             I have assur'd myself of that beforehand,
             And know it will be precious; the thought ravishes.
             (130-2)

indicate recovery of equilibrium and the reassertion of his manipulative intelligence which was revealed earlier in his comments on the meeting of Beatrice and Alsemero. Beatrice believes that she is manipulating him, but all the indications are that it is he who will become the manipulator, as he manipulates her words to have meanings of which she is unaware. It is clear to the audience though not to Beatrice that his reward will be of a sexual nature. His utterance 'Oh, my blood' (146) indicates that Beatrice has released the destructive power of his lust (the word 'blood' had such a meaning in this period). She is unaware of what she has done, remaining confident and complacent enough to think that she has found a simple answer to her problem:

BEATRICE   (aside)   I shall rid myself
             Of two inveterate loathings at one time,
             Piracquo, and his dog-face. (144-6)

The scene ends with a series of references to food and feeding. The expression of De Flores's lust (146) is followed by comparison between sexual appetite and hunger, then, as Alonzo arrives, he is described as 'the man [who] goes supperless to bed,/Yet shall not rise tomorrow to his dinner' (154-5), and there is a final reference at 163 to the fact that ' 'Tis now near dinner time', the time when, it will be recalled from Act I, scene ii, the madmen grew restive and needed to be fed. This scene's linkage of the demands of sex and the appetite for food carries here, as a result of that earlier scene, the additional association of sexual desire with madness. De Flores's lust has been stimulated and he anticipates the approaching satisfaction of his sexual appetite, whilst Beatrice anticipates union with Alsemero.

Act III, Scenes i and ii

Summary

These two short scenes are continuous and so are treated here as one. They take place in the inner recesses of Vermandero's castle. Between the acts De Flores hides a sword ready for the murder. In scene i, as he conducts Alonzo through the castle, he persuades him to remove his sword before they begin the descent through a narrow passage into the vaults. Scene ii takes place in the vaults where De Flores viciously stabs Alonzo three times as he is looking out of a window. De Flores decides to take the diamond ring on the murdered man's finger as proof for Beatrice that the deed has been done. When he is unable to remove the ring, he cuts off the finger.

Commentary

The texture of the writing in these two scenes is less dense than in other main plot scenes, and there are none of the insights into character and motivation found elsewhere in the play. Nor are the scenes strictly necessary to clarify the events of the main plot; the audience know that De Flores is to murder Alonzo, and in Act III, scene iv, he will report to Beatrice that the deed has been done. In a play where every part is carefully worked out, it is pertinent to ask why the dramatists included these scenes of the murder at all. They might simply be there to provide a piece of exciting and sensational action, but they also provide two very striking effects, the one created verbally, the other visually, which contribute to the impact of the whole play on the audience.

Verbally, the setting of Vermandero's castle is strongly conveyed. Earlier references to the structure of the castle are recalled. Alonzo refers to it as 'a most spacious and impregnable fort' (4). Its impregnability is reinforced by the number of keys De Flores must obviously have to take Alonzo round the building (1-3). It seems that every part is locked, and we may recall that in Act I, scene i (166) Vermandero had said about the place 'within are secrets', and there is here the feeling that Alonzo is being shown secret places. It sounds the sort of place in which a murder might be committed without great risk of the body being easily found. The impression is conveyed of a building whose interior has many narrow passages. De Flores persuades Alonzo to hang up his sword in order to make his way with greater ease, and at the end of the previous scene De Flores had spoken of 'the ways and straits/Of some of the passages' (II, ii, 159-60), suggesting a place of many such ways. The idea of a maze or labyrinth is perhaps intended, since the latter word is used twice elsewhere in the play. In Act III, scene iv, Beatrice says 'I'm in a labyrinth' (III, iv, 71), as she tries to understand what will satisfy De Flores as recompense for his action, and Isabella, when disguised as the madwoman, says to Antonio,

> Stand up, thou son of Cretan Dedalus
> And let us tread the lower labyrinth;
> I'll bring thee to the clue. (IV, iii, 110-12)

T. B. Tomlinson (see *Further Reading*) sees a parallel between the labyrinth of the castle in which the murder takes place and 'the labyrinths of sex Isabella enters in the sub-plot' (p. 195). Beatrice also finds herself trapped, as a result of the murder, in a maze of consequences and fears which lead her ever more deeply into sin and towards destruction. Isabella's reference in the above quotation to Daedalus is to the legendary maker of the maze, the Labyrinth, in the palace of Knossos in ancient Crete, at the centre of which was the monster, the Minotaur. The labyrinth leads Alonzo to the heart of Vermandero's castle where he meets his death at De Flores's hand. Beatrice's labyrinth of fears and consequences leads her, too, to De Flores and death. De Flores is viewed by Beatrice as a kind of monster, a loathsome creature, whom she fears, and he is often associated with death in the form of poison, venomous snakes, or tombs (II, ii, 66-7).

If the first of the two scenes verbally conveys a sense of the secrecy of the castle and its intricate maze of passages, the second conveys a sense of a different exterior, the spacious and impregnable fortress to which Alonzo referred. De Flores tells him to look out of a casement and view 'the full strength of the castle' (7) and Alonzo comments on the 'rich variety' (9) and 'Goodly munition' (10). The words make the audience see the outward view at the moment when they are about to witness the murder within. The impression of the fine outward view of the well-defended castle is in contrast to the horrible nature of the crime committed upon the defenceless Alonzo in the darkness of its narrow inner recesses. Thus the two aspects of the castle conveyed here provide a striking mental image of contrasts between outer appearance and the inner reality with which the play is centrally concerned. Within this fortress so fine to the outward view there is blood and the corpse of a murdered man.

The other striking effect of the scenes is a visual one. The lack of thematic detail or insights into character forces the audience to concentrate solely on the event. It is a particularly cowardly act – De Flores stabs the unarmed Alonzo in the back – and it is extremely brutal – De Flores stabs him three times, and then cuts off the finger. The effect is to bring home to the audience the full horror of the crime. Beatrice, who had said to De Flores 'There's horror in my service' (II, ii, 119), has no real conception of what that horror is like; she has not visualised what she has asked him to do. At that moment she was just testing De Flores to see whether he would be prepared to undertake such a task, and she seems to think she will be able to pay him off and forget about it. The audience's experience of the murder places them in a position to appreciate how little Beatrice realises what the pursuit of her desires involves, and elicits horror at her unfeeling and uncomprehending behaviour in Act III, scene iv. These scenes are, therefore, crucial to the critical, moral viewpoint of the play.

The severing of the finger in order to present Beatrice with proof that the deed has been committed not only adds to the gruesome nature of the scene, but makes the audience anticipate the later scene when she will receive it, and they will want to know what her reaction will be.

Act III, Scene iii

Summary

At the madhouse, while Alibius is away on business Lollio follows his master's instructions to keep Isabella behind locked doors. He entertains her by introducing the two latest patients, first Franciscus the madman, who is apparently a poet maddened by love, and then, when Franciscus becomes violent, Antonio, the fool. These two men are actually courtiers who have disguised themselves in order to see Isabella. The madmen off-stage become restive and when Lollio goes out to control them, Antonio reveals that he is a gentleman who has disguised himself as an idiot to gain access to Isabella. He tries to make love to her but she resists. Lollio returns but soon has to attend again to the madmen. Antonio resumes his advances to Isabella, but this time he is seen and overheard by Lollio who appears on an upper level of the stage. The madmen suddenly appear dressed as birds and animals. Lollio takes Antonio away, and, when he returns, attempts to kiss Isabella, revealing that he has overheard what Antonio said to her. Isabella angrily repulses him and warns him to say nothing about what has happened to her husband or she will persuade Antonio to cut his throat. Alibius returns with the news that he has arranged for the fools and madmen to take part in the entertainments which will be presented at the wedding celebrations in Vermandero's castle.

Commentary

The scene begins by stressing the fact that Isabella is being kept in strict confinement to prevent her from being unfaithful to her husband. The terms 'cage' and 'pinfold' (animal pen) are used (3, 8) associating Isabella with a bird or animal thus kept within bounds. The association of human beings with birds and animals is continued in the scene when the madmen appear dressed as such (197). The images of cage and confinement may also be seen as linked to the fortress of the previous scene. A connection is made in the early part of the dialogue between the madhouse and the world outside, which draws the attention of the audience to connections between the main and sub-plots. When Isabella complains that the company she has in the house is that of fools and madmen, Lollio asks 'and where will you find any other, if you should go abroad?' (16-17). All the world, he suggests, consists of fools and madmen. Such a reference must make the audience consider the events which are happening in the world outside the madhouse, and draws attention to a parallel between Beatrice and Isabella. The latter's freedom is literally restricted by the fact that she is kept behind locked doors, whereas Beatrice is not free to do what she wants because of 'the command of parents' (II, ii, 20) and the social and moral ties of her contract to Alonzo. In Act II, scene ii, when she pretends reluctance to tell De Flores what she wishes him to do, she hesitates and sighs and he uses imagery of a prisoner who wishes to be free. 'That sigh would fain have utterance, take pity on't,/And lend it a free word; 'las' how it labours/For liberty!' (II, ii, 104-6). The uttering of the 'free word', Beatrice's terrible command, is thus a breaking out from the confines of morality. Isabella, literally confined, desires liberty and is given a certain amount by being allowed to mix with the inhabitants of the madhouse (38-9), but although she is tempted she does not break out of the moral restriction imposed on her as wife to Alibius despite the fact that Antonio is obviously a much more attractive man than her husband. Lollio says that the new inmate is handsome (26-7) and contrasts the attractiveness of his appearance with his idiocy. The parallel with the main plot where physical beauty is not accompanied by wisdom in the characters of Beatrice and Alsemero is clear.

This scene is full of such parallels. Franciscus, the apparently-insane poet has become mad for love (48-52) and his madness eventually leads him to violence (91). The dialogue between Franciscus and Lollio about changing sex (74-6) recalls the dialogue between Beatrice and De Flores in Act II, scene ii, lines 107-14. Franciscus also refers to being struck blind by Juno (78, 81). Thus, in this section of the scene, love is connected with ideas of madness, blindness, violence and the transforming of one's nature, as happens in the main plot. Here the threat of punishment for the madman who becomes dangerous and attempts to overstep the limits is literally present in the shape of Lollio's whip, which he brandishes; in the main plot the threat of punishment for sin and for ignoring the restrictions imposed by morality is unseen and unheeded largely because characters refuse to acknowledge that their behaviour is sinful.

The section of the scene in which Antonio attempts to make love to Isabella contains even closer parallels. As he reveals that he is not really an idiot, he refers to the power of beauty to transform the lover (127-8). He is one of the changelings in the play and indeed the word 'change' is used as he refers to his real nature (125). He says that he has used the appearance of foolishness to hide the fact that he is a lover (126) but Isabella refers to him four times as a fool (129, 135, 139, 153) and the ironic implication of these references is that his love is foolishness. Antonio's talk of love and the sciences (130-5) may recall the first conversation of Alsemero and Beatrice, and the part of the scene in which Lollio overhears Antonio with Isabella clearly recalls the second meeting in the main plot which is seen by De Flores. Like him, Lollio decides that a woman who has yielded to temptation will prove more amenable to the advances of others, and so he attempts to make advances with the implication that he has power over her since he can reveal all to her husband. The parallel with the main plot is not exact in that the situation here is such that Antonio not only reminds us of Alsemero but also De Flores when Isabella, repelling the advances of Lollio, threatens that if he tells her husband she will see to it that Antonio kills him. She is sure, too, that Antonio is so infatuated he would do it (248-52). In contrast to the main plot, Isabella resists the temptations of love and also counters the threat of blackmail; she is as forceful in her determination to remain faithful to her husband as Beatrice is in her determination to satisfy her desires. Isabella's soliloquy (219-24) underlines the fact that physical restraint, such as locking a woman up, will not prevent her from sinning; her behaviour indicates that only strict adherence to moral principles will prevent it. Though she had begun the scene by desiring freedom, she ends it by agreeing that Alibius had best lock her up (257), thus acknowledging the difficulties of avoiding sin and the necessity for strict restraint.

In this scene, as in Act I, scene ii, the madmen are heard off-stage, a powerful and restive force which threatens to become uncontrollable. Lollio feels the strain of having to look after the madhouse on his own (174-6). The madmen within the house are like hidden human passions which if not kept within bounds are dangerous, as they are shown to be in the main plot. The cry of the madmen 'Catch there, catch the last couple in hell' (171) indicates that they are playing barley-break, a game in which couples ran through a central area called 'hell' and had to avoid being caught. The sound of this game going on at the time when Isabella faces the temptation of a lover in Antonio gives a reminder of the damnation that will be the consequence of sin. The cry is a carefully-placed reference which finds an echo in the main plot when, in the final scene, De Flores speaks of playing barley-break with Beatrice and of them being left in hell (V, iii, 162-3). The appearance of the madmen dressed as birds and animals just at the point when Antonio is tempting Isabella and Lollio, thinking that Alibius will be made a cuckold, whispers 'Cuckoo, cuckoo!' (197), symbolically suggests that madness reduces man to the state of a beast, whilst the connections which the play has made between madness and love further suggest that the transformations effected by love are not transformations to a higher state of being as Alsemero and Antonio present them, but changes which can bring man down to the level of the beast.

The coming together of the main- and sub-plots is anticipated by the news that the madmen and fools are to be present at Beatrice's wedding.

Act III, Scene iv

Summary

Vermandero shows Alsemero round his castle and expresses the wish that he had another daughter whom Alsemero might marry. Beatrice feels pleased with herself for managing to get Alsemero accepted as an honoured guest, and she now awaits the news that Alonzo is dead, quite sure that her father will accept Alsemero as a son-in-law in his place. De Flores arrives, announces that the deed is done, and presents Beatrice with the severed finger. She is shocked and tells him to keep the ring for himself. When she offers De Flores three thousand golden florins he becomes angry. Beatrice does not understand his reaction and naively wonders what will satisfy him as reward. Still thinking he expects money, she says that she will pay whatever he wants but that he must flee. He refuses to go alone, telling her that they are both equally involved in the crime and that she must accompany him. He asks for a kiss from her, and when she stands her distance he makes quite clear that he intends to take her virginity as his reward. He dismisses her appeals to respect her modesty and her high birth by making her realise she has no claim to virtue and is his equal as a result of the murder of Alonzo. She kneels and makes a final plea to him to spare her but he is adamant, and she realises that there is no escape. De Flores embraces her, speaking with gentle and protective reassurance as the scene closes.

Commentary

This scene is the turning-point of the play. Like Act II, scene ii, a major part of it is between Beatrice and De Flores, and our full understanding of the scene comes partly from remembrance of the earlier one. The opening shows Beatrice confident and pleased with her cleverness in devising the means of freeing herself to do as she wants, 'So wisdom by degrees works out her freedom' (13). The audience know she is deluded, and the scene develops from this moment of illusory self-confidence to Beatrice's horrified realisation of her folly, which, far from freeing her, has entrapped her into a relationship with the man she most loathes. At the end of the scene she is a very different woman from the speaker of the first soliloquy. Her self-delusion and lack of understanding of what she has done is evident when she speaks of 'the refulgent virtue of my love' (17). Her love for Alsemero which can only be consummated when a murder has been committed hardly has any claim to virtue, yet she makes claim to virtue, to honour (122) and to modesty (125) until De Flores makes her see that she is as much implicated in crime as he.

The view of herself as wise and virtuous in the first soliloquy is immediately juxtaposed to De Flores's aside, in which the thought of the imminent satisfaction of his lust is expressed through imagery of eating (18), followed by the presentation of the finger to Beatrice. This gruesome token takes Beatrice off her guard and shocks her. Her horrified question 'What hast thou done?' (29) might seem strange as it was she who told him to murder Alonzo, but it conveys the fact that she had not visualised the true horror involved in the deed, which this piece of Alonzo's body suddenly brings home to her with physical immediacy. De Flores's following speech underlines the fact by asking why she should be more shocked by the severing of the finger than by the murder itself.

The presentation of the finger is a moment which is not only horrific but also evokes grim humour. As De Flores's comment indicates, Beatrice's reaction is ridiculous when it was she who asked for the murder to be committed. There is also something ludicrous as well as horrific about the presentation of the finger particularly given the phallic connotations which would have been evident to a contemporary audience. The moment is symbolic in a number of ways. The ring was Beatrice's first gift to Alonzo, an outward sign of her contract to him, and the fact that it will not come off his finger signifies that such a tie cannot easily be broken. There is also a level of sexual symbolism, on which the finger suggests the sexual experience which will be forced upon Beatrice by De Flores. The ring and the finger, suggestive of female and male sexual parts, are inseparable, and may be seen to pre-figure symbolically the inseparability of the relationship of Beatrice and De Flores as a result of the crime. The fact that Beatrice gives De Flores a ring which was the token of her contract to Alonzo indicates that instead of changing her fiancé for Alsemero, she is uniting herself with De Flores. Such a thought is, of course, not in her mind as she gives the ring, and the rich symbolic suggestions of this particular moment are the dramatist's means of making the audience fully aware of the ironies and implications of the situation in a way that the characters are not. They intensify the audience's anticipation of the moment when Beatrice will realise what she has done, and they increase the horrified fascination of the audience as they watch a character unwittingly go to her destruction.

The scene shows a progressive undermining of Beatrice's assumed control of the situation. First she is taken off her guard by the unexpected presentation of the finger, rather as De Flores is taken by surprise at the beginning of the previous interview by Beatrice's unexpected kind words and uncharacteristically gentle behaviour. In the earlier scene, he had gradually emerged from the state of amazement as he acquired a sense of how he might take control of events. In this scene Beatrice does not recover from her initial amazement and horror but becomes increasingly disturbed whilst De Flores correspondingly gains in control. When she has disposed of the ring and the finger she offers him money. It is at this point that the word 'service' recurs (54, 57). The service of the chivalrous lover was not rewarded with money but by the favour of the lady. De Flores behaves in a wounded and affronted manner that Beatrice should treat his action as that of a mere servant who is to be paid (63-5). It is not clear whether his amazement and anger are assumed or whether there is genuine feeling here, but given the complexity of the character-drawing in the play, we should perhaps accept at least an element of the genuine in his sentiments. He is not only angry that Beatrice treats his task as that of a servant rather than of a lover, he also seems to be shocked that she has so little feeling for, or understanding of the enormity and cost to himself of what he has done for her. He speaks twice about his conscience (44, 70), first indicating that the reward of the ring will hardly keep a troubled conscience quiet, and then that he need not have had the deed on his conscience if he had hired someone else to do the murder.

De Flores is not an insensitive character, nor is he amoral as is Beatrice. He can suffer, as we know, under her scorn and anger, and he has an understanding of sin and its effects, as his remarks when he overhears Beatrice and Alsemero show. Later his conscience is indeed troubled by the ghost of Alonzo and the friendliness of Tomazo. So in this scene there is some justification for assuming that, like Beatrice, he has been prepared to commit a horrible crime to gain the love he desires, but that, unlike her, it is with a sense of the sinful nature of what he is doing and of the cost to himself.

Beatrice's asides (71, 75) indicate that she does not understand him and is losing control of the situation. She still desperately tries to offer money, as much as he cares to ask. De Flores then makes clear what it is that he wants with the first of a number of attempts to make Beatrice face her own guilt (83-4). Again the use of the word 'guilty' indicates his understanding of sin and morality, whilst Beatrice's difficulty in comprehending arises from her lack of a moral sense. He demands physical recompense, not at first taking the kiss which will be his initial reward, but asking for it. When she refuses he makes it quite clear that he will force her if she does not kiss him voluntarily (93). The lines suggest that he then tries to do so and that she tries physically to distance herself (101-2). This only makes him more determined, as he finally expresses his determination to take her virginity (115-19). Beatrice's reaction reveals her lack of understanding of him, of herself, and of morality. Taking her virginity, thus murdering her honour, is represented by her as a worse crime than the murder of Alonzo, and she seems to be amazed that De Flores, a man who has just committed a brutal murder, could be wicked enough to rape her. She implies a moral distance between them – she has 'honour' and 'modesty' – which as his dismissive reply indicates, do not exist, 'A woman dipp'd in blood, and talk of modesty!' (126). She is deluding herself, but her mention of sin (127) shows that realisation is dawning. However, having tried to distance herself physically and morally without success, she attempts a further distancing by appealing to the difference in their social standing (130-1), implying that De Flores should behave towards her in a manner more appropriate to his social position. De Flores immediately asserts that they are equals in crime and in a speech which enforces the understanding of sin upon Beatrice with words such as 'conscience' (132) and 'innocency' (139), he makes her see that she has no escape: she is 'the deed's creature' (137). An act which cannot be reversed or changed has been committed and there are consequences arising from that deed which are inescapable. It is as if she has been reborn a different person. De Flores says, 'You must forget your parentage to me' (136). There are two possible levels of suggestion here; it is as if a new Beatrice is born, the child of De Flores and the 'deed' (a union of sin and death) and so she must look upon De Flores as now having the authority of her father, or, just as the woman who marries accepts the authority of her husband over that of her father, so Beatrice must accept the authority of De Flores in the kind of infernal union with him which the 'deed' forces upon her. The understanding of sin is further pointed in this speech by the mention of 'your first condition' (138) which means on one level Beatrice's former innocence, but also may be intended to make the audience think of man's 'first condition' in Paradise before he fell, as a result of eating the fruit of the Tree of Knowledge. That deed had consequences from which no one could escape, and as a result, it was believed, all humankind is equal in its inclination to sin. Beatrice's reaction to this is to attempt a desperate slanging match – 'With thee, foul villain?' (140) – but this only makes De Flores state that she has no modesty – she is a murderess (126) – and no honour – she is a whore (142). She would like to preserve her virginity and her reputation as a virtuous woman but, though she has not yet lost her virginity, she has sinned in her heart by changing her affections. De Flores's threats now reach a climax. If Beatrice refuses to accept the inescapable reality of the situation she has created, and yield herself to him, he will prevent her from marrying Alsemero by revealing the crime and will make her his partner in death if not in life. Beatrice is literally brought to her knees in desperate pleading with De Flores. Earlier in the scene (10) the audience are reminded of the moment in Act II, scene ii when he knelt to her. As she now kneels to him the reversal which has occurred in the relationship is visually emphasised; he now has power over her. Her desperation is evident in that she tries to persuade him to take gold and jewels which he had earlier scornfully refused, and she still talks of 'honour' (158) when she knows it must now be a sham. His implacability comes as little surprise to her and she does nothing more to resist. Acceptance of the situation comes through a clear acknowledgement of sin and its consequences, and another reminder of Original Sin (165). The scene ends in an unexpected and subtle manner as De Flores, no longer insistent, angry and forthright, now raises Beatrice from her knees and embraces her, not with lustful urgency, but gently and protectively. She is overcome with a sense of sin and shame and he will hide this – 'shroud your blushes in my bosom' (167). His words show a sense of her fear and vulnerability – ' 'Las how the turtle pants!' (170) – and he reassures her that she will come to love what she now fears. Having broken her down, he realises that Beatrice needs comfort and protection, and that this is exactly the treatment to draw her close to him.

Act IV, Scene i

Summary

A dumb show, or mime, conveys rapidly that with Alonzo's disappearance, Vermandero has accepted Alsemero as his son-in-law, and that the marriage ceremony has duly taken place. De Flores's cheerful appearance conveys that he has already enjoyed his demanded reward for the murder, but the appearance of Alonzo's ghost, showing the hand with the severed finger, greatly perturbs him.

The scene itself presents Beatrice overcome by fear that Alsemero will discover on her wedding-night that she is not a virgin. Whilst he is out she looks in his room where she finds scientific equipment and a book of experiments. She is particularly perturbed by the fact that he has marked a page which gives details of an experiment for testing whether a woman is pregnant and another for testing for virginity. Worried that Alsemero may try the latter test on her, she thinks of a way of tricking him by having Diaphanta substitute for her in the marriage-bed during the first part of the night. Beatrice pretends she is afraid of sex and says she would give a thousand ducats for someone to take her place. Diaphanta, who has already made remarks about Alsemero's attractiveness, eagerly volunteers. First Beatrice tries the virginity test on her to confirm that she really is a virgin as she says she is. The result is positive and they devise a plan whereby Diaphanta will leave the bedroom at midnight so that Beatrice may take her place.

Commentary

The dumb show is a dramatic means of conveying quickly to the audience that certain events have happened without deflecting attention from the main concern of the rest of the play, which is to show the effects of the 'deed' upon the main characters. We do not need scenes dramatising Vermandero's amazement at the disappearance of Alonzo and his acceptance of Alsemero as a husband for Beatrice, but only to know that such events have happened so that we can concentrate on her degeneration. The appearance of the ghost of Alonzo while the wedding is taking place has a symbolic function. This should have been his wedding and his showing of the hand with the severed finger forcefully emphasises the violent breaking of Beatrice's contract to him. His presence shows that despite the murder and the marriage to Alsemero, Alonzo cannot be forgotten. The effect of his appearance on De Flores suggests that the murderer will indeed be plagued by conscience, and that his joys in his sensual relationship with Beatrice will be no more free from perturbation than her hoped-for joys in the marriage.

The scene begins with Beatrice full of fears. Ironically, in achieving her desire to marry Alsemero she has destroyed the possibility of enjoying what she has achieved. She cannot even spend the first night with him because she is afraid he will discover her loss of virginity and accuse her of impurity and deceit. The first line, 'This fellow has undone me endlessly', indicates her realisation that there is no possibility of ever escaping from the relationship with De Flores, and her sense that she is destined for eternal damnation. She blames De Flores rather than showing any sign of accepting her own responsibility for what has happened. However, the scene presents a Beatrice very different from the girl who so confidently and nonchalantly arranged the murder, unwittingly entrapping herself. Now she is full of fears; the word 'fear' is repeated many times in the scene (2, 53, 64, 68, 72, 75, 81, 96, 125). She now also has a strong sense of the necessity for guile and for thinking out ways of protecting herself. Although she leads Diaphanta on to volunteer to act as her substitute in bed (74–81) rather as she led De Flores on to agree to do the murder, there is the feeling here that she is very much more conscious of what she is doing. The fact that she tries the virginity test on Diaphanta to ensure that she is suitable for the task shows Beatrice carefully ensuring that she will not be caught out. A more consciously calculating woman is emerging under the pressure of the constant threat of discovery. Her fear of discovery is the greater because she genuinely believes that Alsemero is a man of judgement and wisdom (6, 7, 10), who will be able quickly to discover her deceit. However, despite her sense of danger, there seems also a hint that she enjoys taking risks as she uses a gambling image, ' 'Tis a precious craft to play with a false die/Before a cunning gamester' (16–17). Deceiving Alsemero will be a kind of dangerous game; one needs to have special skill (craft) to use the loaded dice while playing with someone who knows all the tricks of the trade. This is a revealing image as it shows that she sees Alsemero as an opponent to be beaten rather than as the partner-in-marriage which she had originally wanted.

When she looks into Alsemero's room, Beatrice, and indeed the audience, discover Alsemero's secrets. Despite the talk about eyes and judgement in Act I, scene i, neither she nor we had known that he is exactly the amateur scientist that the contents of his closet show him to be. The book of experiments which Beatrice finds is called 'Secrets in Nature', and is concerned with the discovery of hidden truths. Many critics have found this scene and the next where Alsemero tries the virginity test on Beatrice ludicrous and out of keeping with the psychological insights into character to be found in the two great scenes between Beatrice and De Flores (II, ii and III, iv) but it is a feature of Middleton's technique in other plays to combine apparent naturalism with stylisation. It is not possible to accept this scene as convincingly naturalistic, but the element of the ludicrous which is certainly present has a purpose. The incongruity between Alsemero's role as lover, his idea that marriage would bring about perfection and the restoration of a paradisal state (I, i, 1–12), and the scepticism of the scientist is evident. Love-values involve faith in the integrity and purity of the beloved, whilst the experiments in the book and Alsemero's apparent interest in them imply thoughts of the possibility of sin and deceit, and the existence of doubt until proof can be established. Such thoughts might seem unworthy of the lover, and the scene serves to question Alsemero's declaration in the first scene that his eyes and judgement were in agreement about Beatrice's qualities. It also shows that for all the talk about love on an intellectual or spiritual level in the first dialogue with Beatrice, and about the transforming nature of love in marriage in the first speech of the play, Alsemero has very basic sexual fears of infidelity. The events of the play show that his fears are justified and that it is wise for him to doubt, but by revealing suddenly and unexpectedly what would appear to be the secret thoughts and concerns of Alsemero and showing their incongruity when set against his professions as a lover, the scene reveals that he is, in a sense, another of the play's changelings. Certainly his stature is reduced by the discovery, and he is seen as little different from other characters in the play.

Diaphanta, in contrast to Beatrice, has no worries about losing her virginity and its effects on her marriage prospects. Her attraction to Alsemero was hinted at in the opening of Act II, scene i, and her aside (57-8) establishes it further. There is an apparent contrast between Diaphanta's directness and sexual suggestiveness (61-3) and Beatrice's assumed modesty, but the audience is aware that the two are similar. It is the sexual attraction that Diaphanta feels for Alsemero and the possibility of satisfying her desires which had seemed impossible that lead her to give no thought to the immoral nature of what is proposed. She is driven by sexual desire like the main characters in the play, and she indicates that as far as her marriage prospects are concerned, husbands pay little attention to virginity if the woman is rich, as Diaphanta will be with the monetary reward Beatrice promises. In fact her social prospects will be improved, 'I'm for a justice now,/I bring a portion with me; I scorn small fools,' (127-8). Her money ('portion') will improve her marriage prospects by attracting suitors of a higher social status than Jasperino, who is, presumably, included among the 'small fools' she scorns. Diaphanta will now set her sights on marrying a magistrate ('a justice').

Act IV, Scene ii

Summary

Alonzo's unexplained disappearance arouses the suspicion that Antonio and Franciscus, who have not been seen for ten days, may have murdered him. Vermandero orders that they be found. When Tomazo enters Vermandero counters his accusations of foul play with the accusation that Alonzo has abandoned Beatrice and thereby insulted the family. Tomazo, believing De Flores to be honest, tries to find out from him who the supposed murderer might be. Alsemero welcomes Tomazo to the wedding, but, believing the new bridegroom to be implicated in his brother's disappearance, Tomazo quarrels with him. Jasperino tells Alsemero of a suspicious conversation between Beatrice and De Flores which he and

Diaphanta have overhead. Alsemero decides to apply the virginity test, but Beatrice fakes the effects and he is reassured.

Commentary

Vermandero is less concerned about Alonzo than with the way that the disappearance of the prospective bridegroom reflects badly on the house and raises public suspicion that he has been murdered. His angry outburst to the servant at the opening is that of a proud man who can only see the situation as it affects himself. He is concerned about his 'honour' (1), that is, his public reputation and integrity. The use of the word recalls Beatrice's concern with her 'honour' and the necessity for preserving reputation (III, iv). Although, when speaking privately to the servant, Vermandero acknowledges that there is the possibility that a murder has been committed in his house (9-14), when he is confronted by Tomazo he adopts the attitude that Alonzo has clearly deserted Beatrice, thus affronting the honour of his house. He refers to the 'honourable love' he showed towards Alonzo and he is angry that all the world should know of the insult; the mention of 'public wrongs' (32) shows just how important to Vermandero are outward appearance and the opinion of the world.

The scene as a whole is concerned with the attempts to discover secrets or hidden truths. Vermandero wishes to find out whether a murder has been committed and whether Antonio and Franciscus are to blame. His language to the servant suggests a legal process: a charge has been brought, warrants for the arrest of suspicious persons will be issued, and they will be arrested and brought to trial. There is necessity for proof. Tomazo, assuming that his brother has been murdered, wishes to take on the role of revenger, but first he has to know who has committed the crime, and so, ironically, he questions De Flores, believing him to be honest. Tomazo assures himself that the proof he needs will eventually be forthcoming. In the final part of the scene the truth of Jasperino's accusation against Beatrice is tested by the virginity experiment, the results of which seem to give Alsemero proof that she is faithful to him. The concern for proofs in this scene is linked to a concern with keeping faith and with honesty. Beatrice's faithfulness is in question, and Vermandero is concerned that in the suspicious circumstances of their disappearance, he cannot in good faith say that Antonio and Franciscus are innocent (11). He is concerned to maintain his integrity and honesty and will not say something which may be untrue. Yet in order to appear publicly as the wronged person and not the wronger, he is prepared to accuse Alonzo of 'breach of faith' (24) and 'infidelity' (28). Vermandero's self-concern is underlined by the irony of accusing the foolishly faithful Alonzo of being untrue. Irony is also present as Tomazo, seeking for the murderer, asks De Flores for information, believing him to be the most honest person in the household. He calls him 'honest' (37), 'kind and true one' (42), 'honest friend' (46), and a man with 'a wondrous honest heart' (57). Tomazo who had been the wise observer in Act II, scene i, when he advised his brother that Beatrice loved someone else, is limited in his ability to see truth when it is masked by cunning deceit. Jasperino, speaking to Alsemero of his relationship with Diaphanta, says he offers 'honest love and she deserves it' (90). After the previous scene such a comment is ironic. Jasperino implies that she deserves honest love because she is virtuous and faithful, but he little knows that she has agreed to give up her virginity in return for money, and that she is now thinking of a marriage of social advancement, to a magistrate at least, rather than a marriage for honest love. The supreme irony in the scene occurs when Alsemero believes he has proved Beatrice's honesty through the use of the virginity test, describing her as 'Chaste as the breath of heaven' (149). The audience have seen that the test actually worked in the previous scene when it was tried on Diaphanta, so its validity is not in question, but Beatrice has knowledge that Diaphanta has not, having read the relevant page in the book and she is able to simulate the effects of the drink so that Alsemero is deceived by appearance. His proof of fidelity rests solely on the testimony of his eyes. The deceptive nature of appearance which is everywhere indicated in the play has just been underlined in this scene by Tomazo's reliance on De Flores's honesty.

Alsemero's behaviour further reduces respect for him. His love for Beatrice is not strong enough for him to question the truth of Jasperino's information. Though Alonzo was foolish to do so, he disregarded Tomazo's similar accusation against the woman he was to marry. Alsemero's immediate reaction is to say that Beatrice will not sleep in his bed, and then he resorts to the virginity test. He is easily deceived, and the incongruity of the undignified and mechanical nature of the test with its effects of sneezing and laughing, set against the high poetic utterance of the last lines of the scene as Alsemero expresses his relief is marked:

> My Joanna,
> Chaste as the breath of heaven, or morning's womb,
> That brings the day forth, thus my love encloses thee. (148-50)

The sudden idealisation of the woman who has just been sneezing and laughing, and the sudden change in Alsemero's language from the prosaic utterance of the scientist to the poetic outburst of the lover, produce a ludicrous effect.

The virginity-test situation and the effect achieved at the end of the scene are close to comedy, despite the fact that this is a moment which might destroy Alsemero's happiness and bring Beatrice to disaster. The virginity test is indeed the kind of situation to be found in the comedies of the period, and Alsemero is reduced by it to being little different from Alibius in the sub-plot, the stock comic-type of the jealous husband concerned to prevent his wife's unfaithfulness. In this scene these features are combined with serious, tragic elements. The treatment of De Flores, in contrast to that of Beatrice and Alsemero, is unambiguously serious. In the dumb show at the beginning of the previous scene, his smile of joy and triumph was stopped by the appearance of the ghost of Alonzo, and in this scene the effect of the murder on his conscience is strongly indicated. The presence of Tomazo reminds De Flores of the murder; he can 'smell his brother's blood' when he comes near (41), and he relives vividly in his memory the moment of killing Alonzo (44-5). Unable to bear to continue the conversation, he makes an excuse to leave, and his final aside indicates how troubled is his conscience (56). De Flores's development is treated from an essentially tragic perspective; he, like Beatrice, cannot escape from the effects of the deed, but the effects on each are different. In this scene there are also moments when a tragic movement is suggested. Alsemero feels that the quarrel with Tomazo on his wedding-day is ominous (78-9); Beatrice feels herself to be in the grip of a kind of fate which compels her to act as she does (124), and Jasperino's line 'Then truth is full of peril' (104) points to the final catastrophe. In the latter part of the scene Beatrice and Alsemero are denied any tragic stature or grandeur, as well as audience sympathy, as a result of the introduction of effects more characteristic of comedy into the serious situation. They are ordinary, self-deluded and foolish people, lacking the noble or heroic qualities of Shakespeare's tragic heroes, and their deaths will be no great loss to the world.

Act IV, Scene iii

Summary

Isabella decides to deal with Franciscus and Antonio. She disguises herself as a madwoman and makes advances to Antonio who repulses her. When she reveals her identity, she tells him that he only loved her for her appearance. Lollio consoles him by telling him that Isabella really loves him and that he can earn her approval by ridding her of a rival lover, Franciscus. Antonio agrees. Lollio then reveals to Franciscus that he (Lollio) knows his real identity, and tells him that he must give some proof of his love for Isabella by getting rid of a rival, Antonio. Franciscus agrees. The madmen and fools rehearse their entertainment for the wedding.

Commentary

This scene, juxtaposed to the last, provides a full commentary on the leading concerns of the main plot. Isabella's comments on the madness and foolishness of love coming immediately after Alsemero's last words as he embraces Beatrice - 'thus my love encloses thee' (IV, ii, 150) - direct the attention of the audience to connections between the two scenes and the two plots. The theme of the deceptive nature of appearance is present with Franciscus's letter, the outside of which, with its 'mad' address to Isabella, hides the true nature of its contents, just as his disguise as a madman hides the fact that he is really sane. Isabella's disguise as a madwoman, which Antonio does not see through, suggests that his love was superficial. He only judged her from the outside and did not love her for the person she was. She scornfully tells him that she has seen through his protestations of love and declarations of her beauty (135-6) and she questions how he can possibly call himself a 'quick-sighted lover' (137). The reference to sight here implies the blindness of love. The dialogue in the scene suggests that even without their disguises as madman and fool, Franciscus and Antonio may be described as mad and foolish. The outside of the letter may be, as Lollio says, 'stark madness', but what is inside he also describes as mad (16, 25) and Franciscus describes himself as mad until he can speak to Isabella. She tells Antonio after he has been tricked by her appearance as the madwoman that he is 'aptly-clad' as a fool (138), and he, in a distraught state at making such a mistake, says he is 'stark mad' (146). The comparison between Beatrice and Isabella which previous scenes have suggested is continued here with a reverse image in which the lady who is beloved appears mad but is in reality sane, whereas Beatrice, who appears sane, is, as her actions show, morally mad. As in the previous scene Alsemero was deceived by his eyes about Beatrice's purity, so in this scene Antonio is deceived by his eyes about the nature of Isabella.

The connections between the two plots are pointed even more directly by reflections of situations in the main plot. Lollio's warning to Isabella that if she falls she will have to grant him sexual favours too, reminds us of De Flores's words in Act II, scene ii, lines 57-60, as he watches the meeting of Beatrice and Alsemero. The preparedness of Antonio and Franciscus to kill their rivals in love, when Lollio tells each of them that this is the means of earning Isabella's favour, reminds us not only of De Flores's preparedness to kill Alonzo for Beatrice, but also of Alsemero's readiness to fight a duel and possibly kill his rival in love. The moral madness which the passion of love engenders will make men willing to kill as proof of their love. The necessity for proof of the truth and faithfulness of the lover is stated by Lollio (195-6). Franciscus in his letter protests that he is 'true and faithful' and this is repeated (14, 169). He must prove this, just as Alsemero was asked by Beatrice in the first scene of the play to prove the truth of his protestations of love.

Madness and love are also linked in this scene through the idea of both as sicknesses to be cured. Franciscus says that he waits for Isabella to cure the madness of his love (27-8), and Lollio suggests that Isabella knows how to cure fools and madmen better than he and his master do (32). Later Lollio tells Franciscus he is likely to be cured of his madness of longing for Isabella and gain the satisfaction of his desires by getting rid of Antonio (188-90).

The main plot has established a concern with honour; Beatrice, Alsemero and Vermandero are all concerned with honour in different ways. This scene contains a piece of dialogue about the nature of honour as Antonio dances for Lollio (92-103). It is a piece of comic commentary which suggests that in society honour is 'but a caper' (101) which cannot long be maintained. The dialogue is immediately followed by Isabella tricking Antonio to maintain her honour, that is, her fidelity and purity. Although she does so in contrast to Beatrice who falls prey to temptation, it is worth noting that there is an element of ambiguity about her words to Antonio. When he does not recognise her and she scorns his superficial love, she leaves with the words 'I came a feigner to return stark mad' (139). It is difficult to know whether she is still maintaining the pretence that she loved him and had really disguised herself to evade 'The nimble eye of watchful jealousy' and is now distraught that he has proved unworthy by not recognising her, or whether there is a hint here of genuine distress at his failure to see through the disguise. The latter would indicate a character who is much more affected by temptation and much nearer to actually falling than if this were all calculated pretence.

Act V, Scene i

Summary

Outside the bridal chamber, Beatrice awaits with increasing anxiety as Diaphanta fails to emerge at midnight as they had arranged. De Flores decides to start a fire in Diaphanta's room to rouse the whole household, so that in the confusion Beatrice can change places with her waiting-woman. Momentarily the ghost of Alonzo appears, disturbing them both. At the cries of 'Fire', Diaphanta hurries from the bedroom and goes to her own room where De Flores shoots her. He returns to announce that the fire has been extinguished but that Diaphanta died in the blaze. Beatrice gives orders for her funeral and persuades her father to reward De Flores for his good service in dealing with the fire.

Commentary

As Act V begins the pace of events quickens. In the previous act Beatrice dealt relatively easily with the threat of discovery through the virginity test, and, with Diaphanta's co-operation, managed to settle her fears about the wedding-night without apparent problems. The threat that she now faces is much greater. There is urgency and, indeed, desperation here. The striking of the clock three times during the scene underlines the passing of time and the urgent necessity of getting Diaphanta out of the bedroom before all is discovered. When De Flores enters, the fact that at first the characters obviously cannot see each other (11-12) emphasises the fact that the scene is taking place in darkness. Later, De Flores notes the rising of the day-star, Phosphorus, announcing that day is near. The fact that the scene is played against this background of darkness about to give way to light underlines in a symbolic manner the threat that Beatrice's dark secret (the word is used in line 6) is about to be revealed.

In the first line Beatrice refers to her fears. Act IV showed that she has not been free from them since she married Alsemero. She has both changed and not changed from the woman she was before the murder of Alonzo.

She is more consciously calculating, as her statement that Diaphanta will have to be killed in order to stop her from revealing all, shows, and there is no attempt to present this deed as anything other than it would be, a coldly-calculated murder. There remains, however, of the former Beatrice the inability to see anything except her own perspective, with the consequent lack of self-knowledge. She considers that Diaphanta is being selfish, having no concern for Beatrice's reputation (4). Her indulgence in sensual pleasures with Beatrice's husband shows that she is nothing more than a prostitute ('strumpet' 2, 64; 'whore' 23) whose lack of ability to control her desires has made her break her word (7). There is sexual jealousy as well as fear here. Beatrice seems unable to see that her words apply to her own case exactly; she could not control her passion for Alsemero and that caused her to break her vow to Alonzo; nor can she see that the relationship with De Flores when she is married to Alsemero makes the word 'whore' applicable to her. She is still concerned with 'honour' (4, 48) but now it is clearly a sham, the appearance of virtue only. The dialogue about 'honour' in the previous scene helps to draw our attention to the word when it is used in this one.

The opening speech reveals just how full of fears Beatrice is, not only for the immediate situation but more generally. She fears discovery but she also lacks security because she begins to be suspicious of others. She thinks that Alsemero's suspicion which led him to apply the virginity test must have arisen because Diaphanta had told him something and when De Flores states that one should never trust a waiting-woman, Beatrice utters the cry of desperation, 'I must trust somebody'. She has destroyed faith and trust herself towards Alonzo and now towards Alsemero, but, ironically, she finds that she needs others to be faithful to her, and that without trust there can be no peace. It is this need, so fully met by De Flores through his quick-wittedness and ingenuity in devising a solution to the problem, which draws the two of them closer together in this scene. If at the end of Act III, scene iv, he adopted a protective attitude towards Beatrice, here he shows it in action, and it is indeed the way to win her to him as her words indicate. For the first time she speaks of loving him, 'I'm forc'd to love thee now,/'Cause thou provid'st so carefully for my honour' (47-8); 'His face loathes one,/But look upon his care, who would not love him?' (70-1). It is a love which arises from the 'service' of the lover (70, 72) but the word applied to the relationship of Beatrice and De Flores now has a level of sexual significance for the audience. Used of De Flores and his actions on Beatrice's behalf, the word becomes 'corrupted' to its baser meaning, and this reflects the corruption of Beatrice herself.

Whilst the scene shows De Flores as ruthless in his protection of Beatrice to the extent of being prepared to kill again, and even to endanger the whole house (33-4), the dramatists continue to indicate that De Flores is troubled by conscience. When Alonzo's ghost appears, De Flores is momentarily disturbed. The day-star which was mentioned earlier must be presumed to be the one source of light in this night-scene, but Alonzo's ghost obscures it, leaving De Flores in darkness. The momentary disturbance is dismissed as 'a mist of conscience' (60), but it is significant that in every scene in which De Flores appears after the murder we are given signs that he is not free from a sense of guilt. Here the urgency of the situation and the necessity for immediate action lead him to dismiss the prompting of conscience quite quickly.

At this moment of tension, Beatrice too sees the ghost, which increases her fear and horror. It may also suggest that her understanding of what she has done and of the consequences of sin is developing more fully. The appearance of the ghost followed by the striking of three o'clock raises her to a pitch of terror, so that the cries of 'fire' come as a partial release of tension and evoke words of love for De Flores, which present the image of the rising sun – 'The east is not more beauteous than his service' (72). The image sustains the audience's sense of time in this scene and is a reminder that the coming of morning light is imminent.

As the scene progresses, the ironies, which began with Beatrice talking about Diaphanta in words which applied to her own case, multiply. The concentration of irony in this scene is one of the factors which contribute both to the audience's sense of the disparity between appearance and reality, and to the mounting tension at the possibility of the discovery of that disparity. Diaphanta, emerging from the bedroom, is told by Beatrice to go to her own room where her reward will follow her; the audience know that the reward will not be the promised money but death (79–80). Beatrice's agreement with her father about the usefulness of De Flores, 'A wondrous necessary man' (91) has a level of meaning unknown to Vermandero. Beatrice's concern about Diaphanta, which publicly appears to be concern about her waiting-woman's safety, is actually anxiety about whether De Flores's plan has worked and she has been killed. De Flores's sorrowful words at Diaphanta's death, 'Oh poor virginity,/Thou has paid dearly for't'! (104–5), whilst on one level apparently a regret that an inno-cent person has died, has a literal meaning which only he, Beatrice and the audience appreciate, for Diaphanta had died because her virginity made her a suitable substitute for Beatrice. The final irony in the scene comes through Beatrice's manipulation. She persuades her father to reward De Flores for his good offices in noticing and dealing with the fire so effic-iently, thus managing to reward him for what he has done for her. De Flores himself appreciates the irony of this and acknowledges Beatrice's cleverness. It shows how she has developed to the point of reaching his own level of subtlety and cunning, and even exceeding it by managing to have the 'last hit'. Moreover, the irony which points up the different levels of awareness in this scene emphasises the closeness of the relationship between Beatrice and De Flores. Gone are all the asides; they now speak directly to each other, sharing their thoughts through ironic comments as they work together to deceive Vermandero and the rest.

42

Act V, Scene ii

Summary

Tomazo, unable to discover his brother's murderer, decides that no one can be trusted. He begins to behave in a disturbed and irrational manner. Deciding that the next man he meets will be the murderer, he strikes De Flores, who, feeling a strong sense of guilt, cannot fight Tomazo, and leaves. Vermandero comes with the news that Franciscus and Antonio have been discovered disguised in the madhouse. It is assumed that they committed the murder of Alonzo.

Commentary

The opening of this scene emphasises further that the murder of Alonzo has been a deed which has destroyed the faith and trust necessary for the civilised conduct of human relationships. Tomazo, unable to discover the murderer, feels that he can trust no one. He has become a changed man, and seems to be on the verge of madness. He had been a sensible and rational man when he advised Alonzo that Beatrice loved someone else, but his failure to discover the murderer leads him to act superstitiously and to believe that the next man he meets will be the villain (6-8). When De Flores enters, he refers to him as 'the fellow that some call honest De Flores' (9), yet he himself had previously regarded De Flores as the only honest man in the castle (IV, i) and attention is drawn to this fact later in this scene (38-9). Ironically, although he is now correct in his judgement, it is merely by chance that he is so, as he becomes increasingly gripped by irrational feelings, not of love like other characters, but of anger and hatred. His words and sentiments are extreme; he holds man's fellowship to be 'A treacherous, bloody friendship' (4), and he renounces 'All league with mankind' (43). Poison-imagery is used in connection with De Flores, appropriately but in exaggerated fashion; if a sword wounded him it would be so poisoned that it could never again be used in an honest fight, and it would have to be thrown away (14-23).

The very irrationality and changeability of Tomazo is further indicated by the fact that when De Flores leaves, he does not maintain his belief that this was indeed his brother's murderer, but acknowledges that he is still in a state of ignorance (46), and when Vermandero brings news of the arrest of Antonio and Franciscus and the suspicious circumstances, he is ready to believe that they are the murderers. There is a certain element of the ridiculous about Tomazo in this scene which derives from his irrationality and the extreme nature of his sentiments. It is as if he too has become infected by the consequences of the 'deed' which has destroyed trust and has provoked passionate feelings of anger and hatred in him.

De Flores comes close to being discovered in this scene as he acknowledges (42), and yet again his sense of guilt and troubled conscience are emphasised. Tomazo's presence recalls to him vividly the image of the bleeding Alonzo (32–3) and De Flores resolves to keep out of his way in future.

At the end of the scene the characters of the main and sub-plots meet on stage for the first time. Providing yet again an example of human fallibility in the perception of truth, both Vermandero and Tomazo believe that Antonio and Franciscus must be the murderers.

Act V, Scene iii

Summary

Alsemero now strongly suspects Beatrice and questions her. She denies adultery with De Flores but admits that she used him to murder Alonzo in order to marry Alsemero. He locks her in his room and confronts De Flores who tells him of Beatrice's corruption. Alsemero sends De Flores in to join her. Vermandero enters with the news that the murderers of Alonzo have been apprehended, but De Flores brings in Beatrice, mortally wounded by him, and before dying she confesses. De Flores kills himself.

Commentary

The opening of the final scene of the play recalls the opening of the first. Alsemero and Jasperino are present and the scene begins with talk about Beatrice who has been observed. In contrast to the vision of beauty and virtue in the church, Beatrice is now under deep suspicion as an adulterous wife. The first line indicates the concern for proof, for the finding of the truth. References to faces and to masks point Alsemero's growing sense of the discrepancy between appearance and reality, and that Beatrice's beautiful face has changed to one of ugliness. The mask image is first used in line 3:

> The black mask
> That so continually was worn upon't
> Condemns her face for ugly ere't be seen.

Here Alsemero refers to what he has seen, the testimony of the eyes, which indicates to his judgement, now, that Beatrice is corrupt, in total contrast to the earlier evidence of his eyes and the operation of his reason in the first scene. The mask-image occurs again when Beatrice maintains her innocence at his accusations and Alsemero says, 'there was a visor/O'er that cunning face, and that became you' (46–7). When he calls her 'whore', Beatrice says that such a word

> blasts a beauty to deformity;
> Upon what face soever that breath falls,
> It strikes it ugly (32–4).

The two references to ugly faces in the first thirty-five lines remind the audience of De Flores, but the references are to Beatrice and point to the fact that she has indeed become like him by becoming his mistress. True beauty, it is implied, resides in integrity of character and this she has lost. Later in the scene Alsemero refers to Beatrice as 'all deform'd!' (77), and at the end he talks of beauty changed to 'ugly whoredom' (197-8). Beatrice's behaviour in the early part of the scene certainly shows her degeneration of character. When Alsemero asks her directly 'Are you honest?' (20) she treats it as a joke at first, laughs, and does not give a direct answer. Alsemero comments on the lack of modesty and seriousness in her reply (21-2). When he confronts her with the fact that Diaphanta had been a witness to her adultery, Beatrice insolently and mockingly points to the fact that his witness is dead, with the implication that he will find it rather difficult to prove his case (57). Alsemero shows that he is very suspicious about Diaphanta's death, and then Beatrice tries to hide her adultery by confessing to the murder of Alonzo. She professes that she is sexually faithful to him but that her love for him led her to stoop to murder. The moral distortion in which murder is made a lesser sin than adultery is evident. Her intention here seems to be to try to throw the guilt for the murder on to Alsemero; it was his love that made her a murderess (64-5); she only did the deed to enable him to marry her, and she reminds him, 'Forget not, sir,/It for your sake was done,' (77-8). It may be that there is even a hint of pride that she has been able to do such terrible things for love. If so, it shows that she is truly on the level of De Flores. Perhaps, too, there is even the feeling that Alsemero may actually praise her and be thankful to her that she has been prepared to risk damnation for his sake. If this is the case, it indicates yet again her inability to gauge other people's reactions, and reveals the totality of her degeneration. She speaks of stroking a serpent for Alsemero's love (66), and later in the scene De Flores calls her 'that broken rib of mankind' (146), a direct reference to Eve, who, according to the Bible, was created by God from Adam's rib. Eve was tempted by Satan in the disguise of the serpent to eat of the forbidden fruit of the Tree of Knowledge, and when she had done so she persuaded Adam also to eat. There is a hint that we are being reminded of this in Beatrice's reference to a serpent as she tries to make Alsemero an accomplice by seeking his approval for the murder. The effect is not what she wishes. Significantly Alsemero acknowledges his first sin as he refers to the time he saw Beatrice in church. Whereas he tried in the first scene to convince himself of the virtue of his love for Beatrice, he now admits that his desires and her beauty 'first unlawfully/Fir'd their devotion and quench'd the right one' (74-5), that is, they distracted him from the spiritual devotion which should have been the purpose of being in church. Now he admits that he had fears about this at the time (76), and the fact that the opening speech of the play was a forced attempt at rationalisation of his actions is confirmed. Then, with apparent confidence, he had asserted his ability to see clearly; now he cries in anguish: 'oh, cunning devils!/How should blind men know you from fair fac'd saints?' (108-9). It is the culmination of the play's treatment of the theme of sight and blindness in relation to the perception of truth. Alsemero now acknowledges that he has been unable to perceive truth, and this inability is a general human failing. He asks how man can tell good from evil when the world is so full of deceptive appearances.

As he sends De Flores into the room where Beatrice is confined, Alsemero has a vision of them both in hell where they will continually act out their 'scene of lust'. The references here to theatrical performance, 'rehearse' (114), 'scene' (115), 'act' and 'audience' (116) remind us of the madmen of the sub-plot who were preparing their performance for the wedding celebrations. The correspondence between them and Beatrice is made a little later when De Flores reveals that while Alsemero slept with Diaphanta: 'I coupled with your mate/At barley-break; now we are left in hell' (162-3), an echo of the madmen who are heard playing the game of barley-break in Act III, scene iii, crying 'Catch there, catch the last couple in hell.' (172). As De Flores admits that he and Beatrice are damned, Vermandero acknowledges that hell is present in that place for all of them (164).

When De Flores brings in the wounded Beatrice, Vermandero expresses his amazement and horror through an image which draws a correspondence between his castle and his daughter (147-8). Earlier in the play, the fortress has been presented as a place which holds secrets that must not be revealed to enemies; it is also the place which holds the dark secret of the murdered Alonzo, whose body is apparently never found. The Castle and the House, as Nicholas Brooke indicates in *Horrid Laughter in Jacobean Tragedy*, (see *Further Reading*) were mediaeval and renaissance emblems of both the world and the human body, and the link between Vermandero's castle and his daughter would have been quite readily apparent or acceptable to the contemporary audience. Beatrice, who should have been a woman of impregnable virtue, has been physically penetrated by De Flores and entered by evil forces, and she has harboured the dark secrets that are now revealed. Vermandero's last words in the play appear to express concern about the dishonour to his family resulting from these events.

At the last Beatrice acknowledges what she is, no longer attempting to deceive herself or others. She uses the image of herself as infected blood which must be taken from the sick person to restore him to health, and must be thrown into the 'common sewer' (150-4). In lines of resounding poetry she then speaks of a fate which tied her to De Flores (154-5), as Alsemero had acknowledged that his fate was decided by his first sight of Beatrice (12). She now recognises her likeness to De Flores which earlier had made her repel him. The image of the meteor is important to the central theme of the play as it was a traditional symbol of change and decay as opposed to the stars which were regarded as permanent and constant. Beatrice now admits her loss of honour (158) and her shame, and there is no attempt to present the situation as anything other than it is, the end of a corrupt life and the death of a 'common thing'. This is no noble tragic death, the image of the infected blood being thrown in the sewer ensures that, but Beatrice dies asking forgiveness of Alsemero.

Though she is not to be admired, she does at least see and acknowledge the truth about herself. De Flores, who had never deceived himself, dies defiantly asserting that he has achieved what he wanted in life by achieving 'her honour's prize', and he shows no fear of death. Despite all the indications of his guilty conscience in earlier scenes, there is no repentance at the end. He is proud to assert that he loved Beatrice and he dies believing that he and she will be united in death. His words suggest that the world cannot touch this pair united by their sin. However, it is Beatrice who has the last word in death, and she cries for forgiveness.

The play ends with the remaining characters facing the truth that has been revealed and facing truths about themselves. Tomazo acknowledges that revenge is unnecessary as there is divine justice. Antonio acknowledges his foolishness, Franciscus his lack of sense, and Alibius – the teacher of madmen – his failure to be a wise husband. The two plots are brought together in the conclusion, linked by a common thematic concern with change and transformation, both destructive and creative, tragic and comic. Evil has been brought to light and purged. Momentarily at least, order seems to have been restored as general clarity of vision is achieved.

3 THEMES AND ISSUES

Although this book has separate sections on characters and themes, it is necessary to bear in mind that this separation is artificial, and is done only to make clear to you the various components that make up the dramatic experience that is *The Changeling*. Character is integrally related to theme as the dramatist chooses particular kinds of characters whose interaction or contrast will forcefully convey the leading ideas or themes of the play; thus for instance, the contrast between Beatrice and Isabella contributes to the audience's understanding of the theme of sin. Major themes are separated here for purposes of clarity but you will notice that they are interconnected and overlapping. For example, the theme of madness is closely related to the concern with sin and the Fall. The summaries of the major themes may be filled out by reference back to the relevant scenes in Section 2.

3.1 CHANGE

The title alerts us to the fact that change will be a major concern of the play. It has a number of meanings, all of which apply to aspects of *The Changeling*. First, the term 'changeling' can simply mean someone who changes, as Beatrice changes in her affections from Alonzo to Alsemero, or Alsemero changes from the restless traveller and scholar to the lover who wishes to stay in Alicante. However, the term may suggest a more radical form of change, which we might call transformation. In the early part of the play Beatrice views De Flores as a loathsome creature, but after the murder she has increasingly to depend on him so that, by Act V, scene i, when he saves her with his plan to set fire to Diaphanta's room and to murder her, he is transformed in Beatrice's eyes to one whom she must love as her protector, and her words, 'The east is not more beauteous than his service' (V, i, 72) indicate the transformation that has taken place in her perception of De Flores. For Alsemero, too, Beatrice is transformed from a creature of beauty and virtue to a woman of hideous ugliness as a result of her sin. The early part of Act V, scene iii has references to the ugly face, first hidden behind a mask (V, iii, 3–5), and then in Beatrice's own words about the blasting of beauty by calumny (V, iii, 32–35). Our attention is drawn to the fact that Beatrice, through her crime and subsequent relationship with De Flores has become like him, metaphorically disfigured and loathsome.

Second, the term 'changeling' can mean a substitute. Alsemero takes Alonzo's place in Beatrice's affections, and later also as her husband. De Flores takes Alsemero's place both in his sexual relationship with Beatrice and as her protector. Diaphanta is a literal substitute when she takes Beatrice's place in the marriage-bed.

Third, the term 'changeling' can mean an idiot, or mentally-defective person. In the list of *dramatis personae* Antonio is referred to as 'the changeling'. For much of the play he pretends to be one of the mentally-defective patients in the madhouse, and when he is tricked by Isabella he realises what a fool he has actually been. One of the functions of the sub-plot is to indicate, through parallels and contrasts, the fact that the people in the world outside the asylum are moral idiots who bring about their own destruction by the ruthless pursuit of their passionate desires without regard to persons and morality. Thus, Beatrice is just as much a changeling in the sense of 'idiot' as in the sense of 'one who changes'.

From all this it will be evident that it is love or lust which brings about the major changes in the play, leads to the substitutions, and makes people act like fools or mad persons. The moon, which, because of its phases, is a symbol of change, is also associated with madness, the word 'lunacy' being derived from the Latin word for moon. The play ends with Alsemero referring to the moon: 'What an opaceous body had that moon/That last chang'd on us!' (V, iii, 196–7). Then he goes on to list the changes that have taken place. The other characters add their changes to the list. You might look through the final speeches in the play and, taking what each character says about the changes that have occurred, think how these are specifically shown in the play. Notice that the changes in the main plot lead to disaster, loss and sorrow – beauty is changed to ugliness, obedience to murder – whereas those in the sub-plot lead to an improvement in the characters and the prospect of a better life – Antonio and Franciscus acknowledge their folly and Alibius is changed from a jealous husband to a more considerate and sensible man. The differences mark the different kinds of ending for tragic and comic modes which the seventeenth-century audience would have expected.

3.2 SIGHT AND BLINDNESS

The play begins with Alsemero seeing Beatrice in church, and the first scene emphasises sight as an important concern of the play. Their first conversation is about the eyes and judgement. Then we learn that Beatrice cannot bear the sight of De Flores, whilst he has to find excuses to see her in order to satisfy his longings. In the second scene Alibius wishes to keep Isabella out of sight of visitors, emphasising that he is aware of the danger that their lust will be engendered through the eyes. The fact that he wishes to keep his wife 'secret' establishes links with the first scene; Vermandero's castle contains secrets which must not be revealed to enemies, and Beatrice hides the secret of her changed affections. In the sub-plot it is literally a matter of Isabella being hidden from view, whilst in the main plot the eyes and the sight are used as metaphors related to the matter of the perception of the inner reality behind the appearance. Alsemero is attracted by Beatrice's outward beauty which he believes must reveal her nature, and the play moves towards the tragic discovery that he was mistaken, which he expresses in terms of blindness: 'oh, cunning devils!/How should blind men know you from fair-fac'd saints?'/(V, iii, 108-9). Characters either refuse to see what is in front of them, as Alonzo refuses to heed Tomazo's warning about Beatrice's lack of love, or they convince themselves that they are capable of perceiving truth and judging character. In both cases they deceive themselves. In Act II, scene i, Beatrice tries to assure herself that she sees with the eyes of judgement (13) as she argues that Alsemero is a more worthy man than Alonzo.

The disguises in the sub-plot express literally the ideas that appearances are deceptive, that man's ability to see truth is limited, and that love which looks only at surface beauty and is not governed by reason can lead to deception both of self and of others. Just as Beatrice figuratively disguises her real nature from Alsemero, so Antonio and Franciscus assume the physical disguise of fool and madman, and Isabella dresses up as a mad-woman to emphasise that Antonio only regards her outward appearance and is quite incapable of knowing her as a person.

The theme of sight and blindness and the perception of truth is expressed in other ways. First, the image of Vermandero's castle, so fine to the outward view but hiding crime and horror within, is forcefully established in Act III, scenes i and ii. The image of the fortress is connected with Beatrice (see Commentary on Act V, scene iii) and the image helps to emphasise the contrast between her outward beauty and her inner corruption. Second, the scene in which Beatrice discovers the book of experiments in Alsemero's room, and the next, in which he tries the virginity test on her (IV, i and ii) emphasise the limitations of human wisdom and perception. Alsemero is presented as a scientist for whom the observation of data and of the results of experiments is an important activity, but he is easily deceived by Beatrice who simulates what she knows is the appropriate reaction of a virgin to such a test. Third the inability of the revenger figure, Tomazo, to discover his brother's murderer shows in another way man's limited ability to discover truth. The concern with secrets links all these points and the play presents the eventual bringing to light of things which were hidden from view.

3.3 SIN AND RETRIBUTION

The main plot shows how one sin inevitably leads to another and to the eventual destruction of the sinner. The play as a whole explores the nature and consequences of sin by suggesting a wider perspective than that offered simply by the main plot. The sub-plot offers a contrasting action in several respects, particularly in presenting Isabella as a woman who is placed in a situation where she might substitute Antonio for her husband, but who, unlike Beatrice, does not succumb to temptation.

The dramatists ensure that the main plot's action is not only seen in conjunction with the sub-plot, but also in relation to the universal human condition by a series of references to the Fall of Man which runs through the play. The story of the Fall is told in the Bible in the Book of Genesis, chapter 3. It tells how Adam and Eve originally lived innocently and happily in the Garden of Eden. God who had created them forbade them to eat of the fruit of the Tree of Knowledge of Good and Evil, but Satan disguised himself as a serpent and tempted Eve to eat the fruit. She succumbed and then persuaded Adam to eat. As a result of this sin, this disobedience of God's command, they were expelled from Eden and became mortal. It was believed that all succeeding generations of the human race, descended from Adam and Eve, were born tainted by Original Sin, with an innate propensity to act in a sinful manner, from which no individual was free.

At the beginning of the play, the dramatists make us think of the Fall when Alsemero talks of 'man's first creation, the place blest' (I, i, 8). He compares the state of marriage with the state of Adam and Eve in Paradise, and speaks as if marriage were able to restore that condition of perfection. What Alsemero omits to consider is that Original Sin prevents man from achieving perfection by his own efforts.

Beatrice is linked with Eve in the final scene when she is called 'that broken rib of mankind' (146), alluding to the biblical story of the creation of Eve from Adam's rib. De Flores is several times linked with the serpent or snake (I, i, 224; III, iv, 165-6; V, iii, 66). In the central scene of the play, the parallel with the Fall and the expulsion from Eden is made explicitly in De Flores's words (III, iv, 137-40). There are also references in the sub-plot. Isabella has some words (IV, iii, 40-1) which may be intended to make such a connection, as may Antonio's lines about picking an apple in the orchard of the Hesperides (III, iii, 181-4). In these lines he refers to a classical – not a biblical – story, that of the golden apples in the garden of the Hesperides which were stolen by Hercules, but the suggestion of plucking forbidden fruit may serve to remind the audience of the biblical story.

The theme of sin and retribution is also developed by setting the action, particularly of the main plot, against references to hell and damnation. Beatrice accepts that in giving herself to De Flores she is eternally damned (IV, i, 1). In the last scene Alsemero sends De Flores to join Beatrice in his closet, saying that they should rehearse the seduction of Beatrice in preparation for the performance with which they will entertain the devils in hell (V, iii, 114–17). The game of barley-break which the madmen are heard playing in Act III, scene iii (172) and to which another reference is made in Act V, scene iii (162–3) involved couples running through an area called hell trying to avoid being caught. De Flores refers to himself and Beatrice playing the game and being left in hell. As Vermandero's next line indicates, they are all in hell. His castle has become a place of torment and horror.

The action of the play is widened through these perspectives to provide an examination of sin and its consequences which has application to the general human condition.

3.4 MADNESS

The theme is stated in a literal form in the sub-plot, but connections and contrasts are made with the main plot. Antonio and Franciscus enter the madhouse from the supposedly sane world outside. Franciscus disguises himself as an insane poet and when Isabella asks Lollio how he became mad, she receives the reply 'For love, mistress' (III, iii, 49). This connection between love and madness is made throughout the play. If madness in the sub-plot is literally presented – apart from the disguised courtiers the inmates of the asylum are actually insane – in the main plot madness is a metaphor. Beatrice may not be literally out of her mind but her over-riding love for Alsemero makes her disregard all moral and social constraints and leads her to embark on a course which will eventually destroy her. Her 'madness' is emphasised by irony. She sets about to rid herself of Alonzo in order to have Alsemero, but by doing so her love is transformed to fear; she has to give herself to the person she most loathes, and she cannot even spend the marriage-night with Alsemero. In her the frenzy of love is changed to a frenzy of fear as she tries in increasingly perilous circumstances to keep the reality of her situation hidden, until she is finally unable to avoid discovery. Thus the main plot equates sin with madness, for it is surely madness to desire the very things which bring about one's destruction. Sin is associated in the play with desire, uncontrolled by reason, and this is the specific madness of the main plot. The game of barley-break in the asylum is only a game, but in the world outside the attempt to escape from being left in hell is serious. In the madhouse the inmates dress up as birds and beasts, expressing quite literally the idea that without reason man is no better than an animal (III, iii, 203–5). In the main plot Beatrice and De Flores become bestial as their desires prompt them; the murder which we see performed is particularly horrible and Alsemero's words in the last scene of the play indicate that Beatrice's beauty has been changed to something monstrous through her actions. The madmen were to perform in the wedding entertainments. As this is not actually shown in the play, some critics have wondered if a scene has been lost. The appearance of the madmen dressed as birds and beasts in III. iii may suggest that these were to be their costumes for the wedding entertainment. The presentation of madmen dressed as animals would have been particularly appropriate for Beatrice's marriage to Alsemero, which was the result of her moral madness, a savage murder, and the supposedly chaste bride's submission to De Flores's lust.

3.5 WHAT IS THE APPEAL OF THE PLAY TODAY?

Though *The Changeling* is in many ways a play of its time, particularly in respect of its mood, its concern with the process of human corruption, and its scenes of sensational horror, it has become increasingly popular with twentieth-century audiences, as the number of professional productions in the past ten years indicates (see *Critical Reception and Approaches*) and it is a play which has received a considerable amount of critical attention It might at first seem surprising that a play which is very much concerned with the theme of sin and retribution, and which has a framework of references to the biblical story of the Fall of Man should appeal to many people today who do not subscribe to the Christian religion and its doctrines. Let us pause to consider why this should be so.

T. S. Eliot expressed the view that *The Changeling* has a moral universality which makes it not simply a play of its times; he said that 'more than any other play except those of Shakespeare [*The Changeling*] has a profound and permanent moral value and horror'. However, it seems unlikely that the contemporary appeal of the play derives solely from its moral values, if, indeed, it derives from them at all.

Twentieth-century audiences have been made particularly receptive to Jacobean plays because much contemporary drama has features, and achieves effects, similar to those found in early seventeenth-century plays. It is significant that both Antonin Artaud (1896–1948) and Bertolt Brecht (1898–1956), whose work has had a profound influence on the twentieth-century theatre, were indebted to Jacobean drama, and critics now make connections between Jacobean and contemporary writers, for instance, Jan Kott in *Shakespeare Our Contemporary* (Methuen, 1965) and Jonathan Dollimore in *Radical Tragedy* (Harvester Press, 1984). Thus, audiences respond, for instance, to the strain of black humour and to the sense of the ludicrous which permeate the tragic action of *The Changeling* with a recognition that derives from their experience of twentieth-century plays.

But there are, perhaps, more specific sources of contemporary interest in the play. It may be that audiences see the predominant sexual interest and the violence of some scenes as being true to life. The events of *The Changeling* are hardly more lurid and sordid than events reported in some of our more sensational newspapers. However, a taste for sex and violence is more likely to be satisfied by the video industry than by a play written

360 years ago, and the contemporary appeal of *The Changeling* lies most probably at a deeper level. It is perhaps significant that whereas the seventeenth-century audiences seem to have enjoyed the play particularly for its comic sub-plot, set in the madhouse, twentieth-century interest has focused upon the main plot and the relationship between Beatrice and De Flores. This is possibly because the modern science of psychology, and in particular the work of Sigmund Freud, has made us more aware of the inner life of the individual and of human sexuality, so that we respond with fascination to a pre-Freudian play which shows such a remarkable intuitive understanding of human psychology, and which admits of interesting psycho-analytic critical interpretations particularly of the relationship of Beatrice and De Flores. For instance, it is possible to see De Flores as not simply a character in his own right but as representing sexuality. At the end of the play Beatrice says: 'Beneath the stars, upon yon meteor/ Ever hung my fate, 'mongst things corruptible' (V, iii, 154–5), suggesting that she could not escape from De Flores, almost as if he were a part of herself. We could interpret her fear and repulsion whenever she sees him in the early part of the play as indicating an inner fear of her own sexual nature, of which, as an adolescent girl, she is becoming aware. When she decides to use De Flores as a murderer she uses her sexual attractiveness to persuade him, and in doing so she releases forces she is unable to control. We note that her attraction to Alsemero, who in her eyes is the antithesis of De Flores, is to a man who, apart from his first kiss of greeting, expresses his love in courtly and spiritual terms rather than with any indication of physical attraction. Beatrice's concern with virginity when she tries to persuade her father to delay the marriage to Alonzo, and also to persuade Diaphanta to substitute for her in the marriage-bed, may not be simply a ploy to obtain what she wants, but may also indicate, at a deeper level, a fear of sex. This is only one way of looking at Beatrice and De Flores, but the fact that such an interpretation is possible for a twentieth-century audience may indicate why *The Changeling* continues to hold our interest today, as may the existence of mythic qualities in the play, with the suggestions of the fable of the beauty and the beast, the conclusion to which is reversed in *The Changeling* with beauty becoming a monster (see Michael Scott, *Renaissance Drama and a Modern Audience* in *Further Reading*).

Finally it is possible that the strong sense of inevitability in the play is a potent source of our fascination. We do not have to hold the same views as Middleton and Rowley on Original Sin and Christian doctrines of damnation and forgiveness to watch with curiosity and horrified fascination as Beatrice becomes more and more hopelessly entangled through her own actions.

3.6 BUT IS IT A TRAGEDY?

Because the tragedies of Shakespeare are probably those with which we are most familiar, our ideas of tragedy tend to be based on our experience of his work. *The Changeling* is very different from Shakespearean tragedy not least because none of the characters possesses admirable or noble qualities, and there is therefore no sense of tragic loss as there is even in a play such as Shakespeare's *Macbeth* where the hero is a murderer. This probably raises in our minds the question whether *The Changeling* is a tragedy at all. What we have to recognise is that Middleton and Rowley's vision of life as expressed in their play is different from the view we find in Shakespeare's tragedies. Middleton and Rowley present not the tragedy of an individual but a tragic view of human life in general: human reason is limited and all people have an innate tendency to sin, so that, without holding fast to moral principles, they are likely, blindly, to bring about their own destruction. Because Beatrice and Alsemero are not exceptional persons, and are no different from others by reason of their great virtues or noble qualities, we see them as more like ourselves and are invited to see in them an example of the general human condition. The frequent references to the Fall of Man reinforce this.

The action of *The Changeling* has an inevitability which is important to the creation of tragic effect. Once Beatrice has had De Flores murder Alonzo, an irreversible set of consequences is set in train, just as it is when Macbeth murders King Duncan in Shakespeare's tragedy. Moreover, dramatic irony – by which a speaker is unaware of the significance of what he or she is saying, or by which actions have a significance for the audience uncomprehended by the characters – is a strong feature of *The Changeling*, as it is of many of the greatest examples of tragedy in world literature, for example Sophocles's *King Oedipus* (fifth century BC) and Shakespeare's *Macbeth* (1606). *The Changeling* powerfully presents the tragic spectacle of a woman unwittingly bringing about her own destruction, and, though she is not admirable, nor even very likeable, the audience watches in horror.

4 TECHNICAL FEATURES

4.1 CHARACTERISATION

The central focus of *The Changeling* is the relationship of Beatrice and De Flores. These two characters are presented with a fullness of detail, and a degree of psychological realism lacking in the presentation of the other characters. In the play as a whole the degree of characterisation varies considerably. The other characters serve as means by which Beatrice, De Flores and their actions are highlighted and understood, and the dramatists' treatment of them varies according to their function. Alsemero and Vermandero who are closely involved in the main action are not as fully developed as Beatrice and De Flores, but some complexities of character and individual details are suggested. In contrast, there are a number of dramatic types; Tomazo, the revenger, Alibius, the foolish, jealous husband, and Lollio, the comic servant, who would have been familiar to the audience from innumerable plays of the period. The characters of the sub-plot are not developed. Isabella serves as a contrast to Beatrice, whilst Antonio and Franciscus are simply examples of the foolishness into which men can be led by love. These examples serve to establish and reinforce a point of view on the actions of the main plot.

Beatrice-Joanna

The first appearance of Beatrice shows her poised and socially assured. She is not taken aback by the public kiss of a man she has never met before and has only seen at a distance in church. She handles the situation with remarkable ease and confidence, and the assumption must be that she feels about Alsemero as he does about her. She recognises him as a scholar, a searcher after truth, and she suits her language to him by talking of love and the sciences. There is an element of flirtatiousness in the way she leads him on to declare his love and avouch its truth.

From the start Beatrice is a manipulator, using her attractiveness and socially-charming manner to make people say or do what she wants. She uses this ability most obviously on De Flores in Act II, scene ii, leading him on by treating him gently and kindly, touching him, calling him 'my De Flores', and getting him to demand what he should do for her. Less importantly and less directly, she persuades her father to delay the marriage to Alonzo by three days (II, i). She also, by indirect means, leads Diaphanta to volunteer to substitute for her on the wedding-night. When she does not keep to the arrangement, Beatrice is finally at a loss and has to rely on De Flores to retrieve the situation by starting a fire, but by the end of the scene she has recovered enough to manipulate her father to give De Flores a reward. Even at the last she tries to manipulate Alsemero, as she has done earlier with the virginity test, by telling him that it was for his sake she had Alonzo killed, as if she expects him to collude with her in keeping the secret (V, iii, 65-72). This is a miscalculation, just as she miscalculates with De Flores.

These disastrous miscalculations show that although she is a manipulator, Beatrice is not a mature, clear-headed schemer like De Flores. She knows how to get her way be being charming and appealing, and it has been suggested that there is much of the spoilt child about her, determined to have what she wants. Her reactions to De Flores in the first scene show that she is not quite the poised and mature person she might have appeared in her dialogue with Alsemero. Her calm and assured manner is disturbed by De Flores's appearance; she becomes agitated, revealing in words and manner inner insecurities, and – particularly in the incident with the gloves at the end of the scene – an unpleasant side to her nature. It is not clear whether the first glove was dropped by accident or as a love-token for Alsemero to retrieve. If it was so intended, her reaction to De Flores's retrieval of the glove is very much the petulance and even viciousness of the child who has not managed to get her way. Like a child, Beatrice is self-centred and naive, for all her apparent knowingness. She seems to have reached an age at which she realises that her physical attractiveness gives her power to persuade men to do what she wants, but she lacks the experience which would make her realise what turbulent and dangerous forces she can release by her actions.

It is not only lack of experience of life which makes Beatrice unaware of the consequences of what she is doing. She is so self-centred, seeing everything in terms of herself and her own advantage, that she takes no thought for what others may feel. She uses other people, like De Flores and Diaphanta, quite ruthlessly for her own ends, and when they show that they have some desires of their own and are capable of independent action, Beatrice is shocked. She regards people as wicked when they do something which hurts her whilst she fails to see that she is no different from them in her own actions (for example, III, iv, 120-2). It is this failure to understand other people because of her self-centredness which in large measure brings about her downfall. She sees everything purely in her own terms and her lack of imagination prevents her from envisaging what the murder would be like, so that she is extremely shocked when the reality is forced upon her in the shape of the severed finger. For her the killing of Alonzo is simply the removal of an obstacle to her happiness, and as long as it is removed she does not concern herself with what is involved. At the beginning of the play her fear of De Flores suggests an intuitive sense of the danger he presents, but she suppresses this in order to pursue her desires. Beatrice is thus utterly amoral; she has no moral sense of right and wrong, and therefore no sense of sin and guilt. In this she is different from the immoral De Flores who consciously pursues the path of sin and suffers from pangs of conscience. It is very noticeable that for most of the play Beatrice refuses to acknowledge that she is no longer virtuous. In Act III, scene iv, she talks of her honour and modesty and De Flores has to confront her with the illogical and ridiculous nature of the assertion, 'A woman dipp'd in blood, and talk of modesty!' (126). In Act V, scene i, as she waits for Diaphanta to emerge from the bedroom, Beatrice still talks of honour (4, 48) but it is very clear that she is referring to her public reputation, the preservation of the appearance of virtue without the inner reality.

We have a sense of Beatrice becoming more and more desperate to preserve the secret of her corruption after the murder as she meets a series of situations in which she is increasingly in danger of discovery, first the virginity test, then Diaphanta's failure to leave the bedroom as arranged, and finally Alsemero's direct accusation in Act V, scene iii. Even in the last situation she still refuses to confront her own sin and responsibility, as she tries to put the blame on Alsemero: 'your love has made me/A cruel murd'ress' (V, iii, 64-5). It is not until the last moments of the play, as she is dying that Beatrice acknowledges her corruption (V, iii, 150-3). She finally admits that she has no honour as she says of De Flores, 'Mine honour fell with him, and now my life' (V, iii, 158), and she dies asking Alsemero for forgiveness (V, iii, 178-9).

Isabella

Isabella, the wife of the madhouse doctor, Alibius, is presented as a contrast to Beatrice in the main plot. She has a forceful nature and chafes against the restrictions her husband puts on her, but she does not take the freedom to do as she wants as Beatrice does. Even when Antonio and Franciscus present themselves as rather more attractive lovers than her foolish husband, she does not fall prey to temptation, but makes fools of them. Unlike Beatrice, she sees things clearly and is able to act in a morally-decisive manner, although when she tricks Antonio by disguising herself as a madwoman there is a certain ambiguity about her words as she leaves (IV, iii, 139) which suggests that perhaps she is distressed that he did not recognise her in her disguise. We are left with a hint that she was attracted to him and might have given in to his advances had he not revealed that his love was simply for her appearance.

Whereas Beatrice is unable to deal with De Flores's blackmail because she has given in to temptation, Isabella's resistance allows her to prevent Lollio from being a threat in Act III, scene iii when he overhears Antonio's love-talk. She angrily defies his attempt to kiss her and blackmail her, and she does so with a hint of ruthlessness which reminds us of Beatrice:

> be silent, mute,
> Mute as a statue, or his injunction,
> For me enjoying, shall be to cut thy throat; (III, iii, 248–50).

De Flores

De Flores is the most interesting character in the play. In his early appearances he is not a plotter, nor indeed is he capable of achieving by his own efforts what he most desires. He is a gentleman who is in service to Vermandero and is respected and relied upon by him. De Flores is apparently impoverished as he refers to his need for money when Beatrice offers him financial reward (III, iv, 111–12). This is perhaps the reason he has a subservient role in Vermandero's household. It is clear that there is a great difference in social status between him and Beatrice; one of the ploys she uses to fend him off as he demands his sexual reward for the murder is to remind him of his lowly status compared with her (III, iv, 130–1). This difference in social status combined with the disfiguring skin rash makes the fulfilment of his desire for Beatrice very unlikely in the early part of the play. He is frustrated, a victim of uncontrollable passions which cause him great suffering. Middleton presents De Flores's condition as like an addiction: he has to see Beatrice with increasing frequency to satisfy his longing (II, i, 29–31). Thus he is established as just as much in the grip of passion as Beatrice or Alsemero, and determined eventually to have his will, as the last line of the first scene indicates.

Despite his suffering De Flores has an inner resilience and a sharply cynical sense of humour which make him a fascinating and even entertaining character for the audience. His ability to see his own situation clearly and to smile wryly at the ridiculousness of his behaviour: 'Why, am not I an ass to devise ways/Thus to be rail'd at' (II, i, 77–8) reveals a clear-sightedness which is in contrast to the self-deceptions of Alsemero and Beatrice. He can joke about his appearance. He has observed human behaviour and he knows that worse-looking men than he have had success as lovers; the observation is expressed in images that are exaggerated and grotesquely comical as he describes how men with hardly a beard are doted on (II, i, 40–7). The reaction of the audience is usually to laugh at the comparisons in these lines, and this vein of humour – which is completely lacking in Beatrice and Alsemero – makes De Flores an attractive dramatic character, whilst at the same time the audience recognise him as dangerous.

The extraordinary complexity of De Flores's character is indicated by the changes of mood to be found in the two central scenes with Beatrice. In Act II, scene ii, he moves from bewildered ecstasy as Beatrice greets him kindly and touches him, to developing awareness of how he might use the situation to his own advantage. Act III, scene iv, shows him moving from polite greeting of Beatrice, through developing anger as she offers him money and growing insistence on the satisfaction of his desires, to forthright forcing of Beatrice to confront what she has done, reducing her to a state of helpless pleading, at which point De Flores finally enfolds her in a protective embrace with quietly-reassuring words. The complexity of the character is further developed by the recurring expressions of guilty conscience. De Flores has a moral sense, but he is prepared to do evil because of his overwhelming passion for Beatrice. He is shocked that she does not appreciate the enormity of what he has done for her sake, and tells her that he could have hired someone else to commit the murder (III, iv, 68-70). The violent moment of murdering Alonzo is imprinted on his memory and he recalls it with a vividness that disturbs him extremely when he meets Tomazo in Act IV, scene ii, and again in Act V, scene ii. He is also troubled by the appearances of Alonzo's ghost. These moments of conscience are nevertheless controlled by his resilient and resolute will. He is resourceful in dealing with the problem of getting Diaphanta out of the bedroom and he is only momentarily troubled by the appearance of the ghost (V, i, 58-60) so that by the end of the scene, with the task successfully completed, he is able to laugh at Beatrice's ingenuity in obtaining a reward for him.

In the final scene, when confronted by Alsemero with the knowledge that all has been revealed, De Flores, unlike Beatrice, does not try desperately to deceive still further, nor does he lament or curse. He shows a stoical resilience, and calmly enters Alsemero's room, mortally wounds Beatrice and finally kills himself, though not before he has defiantly asserted that he has loved and enjoyed Beatrice. It is as if death holds no fears for him, and as if in achieving his desires his life had been a fulfilled one which he can leave without regret (V, iii, 167-71). Beatrice has been all his, and, now he has killed her, they will be together in death (V, iii, 175-7). We may admire the strength and bravery of his defiance of the world and its moral systems as he meets death, whilst at the same time being horrified at the wickedness of his actions and recognising the strength and defiance as consistent with the ruthlessness and cynicism he has shown elsewhere.

Alsemero

When we first see him, we may expect that Alsemero will be the hero of this tragedy, but the dramatists establish little about him to make him particularly attractive, or a character with qualities which raise him above others in the play, any more than Beatrice is an attractive or nobly virtuous woman. The attempt to justify his feelings in the opening speech of Act I, scene i, hints perhaps at weakness, or at least naivety as his later words and actions show. Jasperino stresses that Alsemero is totally inexperienced in the ways of love, and his behaviour bears this out. His directness with Beatrice when he first meets her might seem to demonstrate resolution and the strength of his attraction to her, but it also shows his lack of experience of wooing women. Later, his reaction to Beatrice's words about Alonzo in Act II, scene i, that he will challenge him to a duel seems to be based on a sense of how the lover ought to behave gained perhaps from reading love-stories rather than from a sensible appraisal of the situation, as Beatrice's response indicates when she points out the likely results of such an action. The realism of her objection undercuts Alsemero's fine, heroic sentiments and makes him look slightly ridiculous. Indeed, at no point before the final scene do the dramatists allow Alsemero to assume anything like a noble or heroic stance.

He is first represented as a restless traveller, and Beatrice's words at their meeting suggest that he is a scholar. The impression of him as a searcher after truth and knowledge is borne out by the discovery of the secrets of his study by Beatrice. The book, *Secrets in Nature*, suggests deeply serious enquiry into the nature of the world and of human existence, and Beatrice says, 'Sure he does practise physic for his own use,/Which may be safely call'd your great man's wisdom.' (IV, i, 22–3). The suggestion that Alsemero is a wise man concerned with high matters is not continued for long. When Beatrice looks at the pages he has marked, she finds experiments which test for pregnancy and virginity, and which suggest that Alsemero is as concerned as everyone else with sexual matters. The parallel is immediately drawn with Alibius, Isabella's jealous husband who is concerned to keep his wife faithful to him. He is a doctor and Alsemero's room is described by Beatrice as 'A right physician's closet' (IV, i, 20). Such a parallel with the comic type of the jealous husband reduces Alsemero's stature immediately and makes him seem ridiculous. It also suggests that for all his courtliness, he has sexual doubts and fears about Beatrice. His stature is further reduced when he applies the virginity test and is deceived by Beatrice. As he thinks he has proved her to be faithful and a virgin, he starts to talk again in an elevated poetic style which must seem to the audience ludicrous because of the ironic nature of the words:

> My Joanna,
> Chaste as the breath of heaven, or morning's womb,
> That brings the day forth, thus my love encloses thee. (IV, ii, 148–50)

What Middleton and Rowley seem to be stressing in their presentation of Alsemero is man's inability to find or see the truth, and it is this which Alsemero eventually has to acknowledge in: 'oh cunning devils!/How should blind men know you from fair-fac'd saints?' (V, iii, 108–9). When he finally acknowledges this fact about himself, and that he is in this respect like everyone else, he begins to regain some strength and seriousness, acting decisively in dealing with Beatrice and De Flores, and bringing the play to a close with a voice of authority.

The dramatists are primarily concerned with exploring the relationship between Beatrice and De Flores, and the character of Alsemero is not presented in as much depth nor developed as fully as theirs are. He is important in so far as he affects Beatrice's actions. We understand him and De Flores more fully by the contrast which the dramatists establish between them. The self-deception, courtliness and blindness of the one highlights the clear-sightedness, bawdy forthrightness and cynical realism of the other.

Vermandero

Vermandero is Beatrice's father and governor of the fortress at Alicante. He is established as a haughty man who is determined to have his way in marrying his daughter to the nobleman, Alonzo de Piracquo. One gains the impression that Beatrice had had little say in the matter, but that until she met Alsemero she had been happy to go along with her father's wishes. Vermandero shows little concern for others' feelings and great concern for his own pride and honour. When Beatrice first tries to persuade him to delay the marriage and uses the argument that she wishes to remain a virgin a little longer, he dismisses her with words, 'Tush, tush! There's a toy' (I, i, 197). He shows little sensitivity towards her feelings, though in Act II, scene i, he does accede to her request and delays the marriage by three days, suggesting that perhaps he is an indulgent father as well as being determined to have his will. The impression we receive of Vermandero is of exactly the sort of man who might have as his daughter the spoilt and wilful Beatrice.

In the latter part of the play Vermandero is more concerned about how the disappearance of Alonzo may reflect on his reputation and honour than about Alonzo himself or his brother, Tomazo. Even at the end of the play, with his daughter dead, his immediate reaction is not to mourn for her but to be concerned about how the scandalous events affect his own reputation. His last words are a lament: 'Oh, my name is enter'd now in that record,/Where till this fatal hour 'twas never read' (V, iii, 180–1).

Vermandero's concern for honour and reputation is expressed dramatically through the image of the fortress, of which he is so proud and which seems so impregnable, and the correspondence drawn in the play between the fortress and Beatrice. When she introduces Alsemero to her father, Beatrice presents him as a gentleman who is 'desirous/To see your castle' (I, i, 159–60), knowing that the way to get her new lover into her father's favour is for him to show an interest in the fortress. In the last scene, as the wounded Beatrice enters, Vermandero cries: 'An host of enemies enter'd my citadel/Could not amaze like this: Joanna! Beatrice-Joanna!' (V, iii, 147–8). The fortress and his daughter are the two things most precious to him and which he believes are secure. The honour of his family is to be enhanced by the socially-advantageous marriage to Alonzo but

Beatrice carries within her character the propensity to sin which will undermine the house as surely as if enemies had invaded the castle. For Vermandero the castle in which he delighted is transformed to hell itself (V, iii, 164).

Alonzo De Piracquo

Alonzo appears briefly in the play, but he is more important for what he represents than as a fully-developed character. He is a nobleman and there is no reason for us to feel that he would be anything other than a good and suitable husband for Beatrice. When his brother, Tomazo, tries to persuade him to break off the match because Beatrice clearly does not love him (II, i, 123-52) Alonzo refuses to believe ill of her. He utters honourable sentiments and would protect his future wife from calumny, but the dramatists show that he is foolish to be so trusting. He is as much determined to have his will and to marry Beatrice, as she, Vermandero and De Flores are determined to have theirs, and he will not listen to what he does not want to hear, thus deluding himself fatally.

His next appearances are at the end of Act II, scene ii, and in the following scenes, Act III, scenes i and ii, which lead to, and show, his murder. Here he is seen as a victim, butchered most horribly to satisfy both Beatrice's desire for Alsemero and De Flores's lust. His subsequent appearances as a ghost (IV, i, dumbshow; V, i, 58-61) emphasise the wrongfulness of the act. It is not only the killing of an innocent man, but also represents the forcible breaking of solemn vows. When Beatrice's ring will not come off Alonzo's finger, the point is made symbolically that such promises cannot so easily be broken.

Alonzo is contrasted with Alsemero, who becomes a substitute for him. Though Beatrice in Act II, scene ii, presents Alonzo as someone unpleasant whom she does not want to kiss (16-18) the audience know otherwise and contrasts are established with Alsemero, whose behaviour must appear questionable in view of the fact that he knows of Beatrice's engagement but persists in pursuing his interest in her. A contrast is also established with De Flores whose repulsive face Beatrice will touch later in the scene in her attempt to persuade him to commit murder.

Tomazo De Piracquo

Tomazo is not a developed character. He is the familiar dramatic type found in the drama of the period, the revenger, but he is presented in a different perspective from most revengers in other plays (see Section 1.5).

Diaphanta

Diaphanta is first heard in the bawdy conversation with Jasperino in the first scene (137-52). He makes suggestions to her which she fends off in an amused fashion, knowing exactly what he means. She expresses an attraction for Alsemero at the opening of Act II, scene ii, and later in Act IV, scene i (57-8). In the latter scene she has a sexually-suggestive speech which makes Beatrice exclaim 'I fear thou art not modest, Diaphanta' (IV, i, 59-64). She is quick to volunteer to take Beatrice's place in the marriage-bed and slow to leave it when she is there. All these words and actions indicate that Diaphanta is a woman who does not attempt to hide her lustful nature. In this she is contrasted with Beatrice who continually attempts to present her feelings for Alsemero as on a higher plane, and deludes herself about their nature. Diaphanta, as the substitute for Beatrice on the wedding-night, is another of the changelings in the play.

Alibius and Lollio

These two are stock comic characters. Alibius is the type of jealous husband who desperately tries to make sure that his attractive young wife is not unfaithful to him. This type of character appears in many comedies of the period. Lollio is a type of the comic servant whose humour more often derives from playing with words than from actions. He is not a foolish or stupid character, since he, like De Flores whom he mirrors, sees that he will be able to enjoy his desires if Isabella gives in to temptation.

4.2 VERBAL RECURRENCE

Middleton's dramatic style is plainer and more economic than that of Shakespeare or of his contemporary, John Webster. In *The Changeling* there is some connective tissue of verbal images of poison and of references to the Fall, but there is a much less fully-sustained and developed pattern of iterative imagery than is to be found in Shakespeare's work. Images are used but usually for strong isolated effects as in the lines: 'The bed itself's a charnel, the sheets shrouds/For murder'd carcasses' (V, iii, 83-4). The central dramatic metaphors of sight and madness are expressed more through the verbal recurrence of words such as 'eyes', 'madman' or 'fool' than through striking images. In all his plays Middleton alerts his audience to his central concerns in this way. In *The Changeling* the word 'change' is clearly important, as is 'secret' (for example, I, i, 166; I, ii, 1, 2, 7, 16; II, ii, 68; IV, i, 25; IV, ii, 139). Words such as 'faith' and 'honour' are significantly repeated and sometimes there is a concentration of particular words in certain scenes, which may give an indication of the scene's central focus. In the case of 'honour', the changing emphasis of its meaning from 'personal integrity', signifying wholeness and correspondence between what a person appears to be and what he or she is, to 'reputation' in the sense simply of exterior appearance and report, reflects on a verbal level not only the corruption of the concept of honour but also the corruption of Beatrice.

The most noticeable example of verbal reiteration is of the word 'service', meaning on one level honourable deeds performed by the chivalrous lover for his lady, and on another level sexual intercourse. Act II, scene ii has a particularly large number of references to service. Between Beatrice and Alsemero the word denotes the honourable actions of the lover on behalf of the lady, but as the section of the scene between Beatrice and De Flores progresses and he begins to realise that he has the opportunity to achieve his desires, the word begins to gather sexual suggestion. Beatrice, in talking to De Flores of 'service', treats him as if he were a lover being sent off to perform some honourable deed to show his love for her, but the deed is a murder, and, in playing with the idea of service for her own ends, Beatrice is perverting it. The word recurs again significantly in Act V, scene i, when Beatrice, relieved at De Flores's quick thinking and action in starting the fire, talks of his protecting her 'honour' and exclaims, 'The east is not more beauteous than his service' (72). De Flores, like the chivalrous lover, protects the lady's honour against calumny, but, just as the honour of Beatrice has come to mean nothing more than surface reputation, hiding the evil and rottenness within, so the word 'service' reminds the audience that the relationship of Beatrice and De Flores is one of lust and physical degradation. The reiteration of the word throughout the play and its change of meaning reflect on a verbal level the development and transformation of Beatrice from a woman associated with high hopes and ideals to a 'common thing'.

4.3 VISUAL IMAGES

You should remember that *The Changeling* is a play, written for performance in a theatre. The text contains innumerable signs related to its physical realisation on stage. The visual dimension can be as important as the verbal in the theatre, and as you read you need to try to envisage what the audience would see as well as paying attention to the words they would hear. Middleton often sums up the significance of a scene or phase of the play in a striking moment of symbolic action in which verbal and visual elements combine to convey to the audience in concentrated form the essence of what they are witnessing.

The most memorable and powerful of such moments occurs in Act III, scene iv, when De Flores presents Beatrice with Alonzo's severed finger. This reminds the audience of the horror of the murder which they witnessed in Act III, scene ii, and in a literal way it forces Beatrice to confront the physical reality of the crime she had not troubled to envisage. On a symbolic level, as the Commentary (Section 2) on this scene indicates more fully, the image of the finger and ring simultaneously suggests not only Beatrice's tie by vow to Alonzo which cannot so easily be broken but also De Flores's sexual intentions towards her and the fact that, though she does not realise it, the deed will cause De Flores to be a substitute for

Alonzo. Thus in a concentrated moment of action in which a visual image is of central importance, Middleton draws together past (the murder), present (De Flores's sexual intention) and future (the relationship between Beatrice and De Flores) so that the audience are aware of the full significance of what they are witnessing. During this brief piece of action the ring is transformed from the honourable symbol of Beatrice's betrothal to an obscene symbol of sexuality.

Famous as this moment in the play is, it is not the only one of such dramatically powerful symbolic incidents. At the end of the first scene Beatrice drops a glove (I, i, 225); Vermandero notices and instructs De Flores to pick it up; when he does so Beatrice is angry and throws down the other glove, vowing that she will never wear them again now that he has touched them. Her anger at De Flores's 'officious forwardness' (227) suggests that she would have wished Alsemero to retrieve the glove. What the audience see are two different gestures: one glove is dropped, the other thrown down. Throwing down a glove is the traditional sign of a challenge to combat, whilst dropping a handkerchief, scarf or glove was often a sign of a lady's favour towards a lover, who would retrieve it and wear it. Gloves and scarves appear as love-tokens in Elizabethan poetry and in earlier times such tokens might be worn in the knight's helmet or on his arm. So Beatrice's first glove may have been such a favour intended for Alsemero. Throwing down the other glove obviously is not a gesture that Beatrice literally intends to fight De Flores, but is simply an action of defiance and impetuous anger; however the audience may read it as a sign from the dramatist of the future conflict between these characters. As he speaks his final words, De Flores thrusts his hands into the gloves and what began as a love-token dropped by a lady for her lover becomes the object of an obscene gesture which symbolises De Flores's lustful desire for Beatrice and prefigures what will actually happen. His last speech shows that he is taking up her 'challenge'. He will vex her with his constant presence and is determined to have his will. This moment which depends greatly on visual signs sums up the situation for the audience, and provides psychological insights. The transformation of the token of love to an object of lust provides yet another of the instances of change or transformation to baseness which are at the centre of the play.

Another important visual moment is the murder itself in Act III, scene ii. Verbally the scene builds up an image of the magnificent exterior of the castle whilst visually we are presented with an horrific murder. If you look back to the Commentary in Section 2 you will find this point given more detailed treatment.

The change in the relationship of Beatrice and De Flores as a result of this deed is pointed visually by the fact that in Act II, scene ii, he kneels to her to tell him what service she wishes him to perform, and in Act III, scene iv, she kneels to him imploring him not to take her virginity. Our attention is drawn to this reversal by the fact that we are reminded of the earlier scene as De Flores recalls how he 'sued and kneel'd' (110) to be told her wishes. The reversal of the visual image in these scenes indicates the shift of power within the relationship. In Act II, scene ii, Beatrice is dominant and has manipulative control, but by the end of Act III, scene iv, De Flores has gained power over her. It is he who stands as she grovels, and it is he who raises her up and draws into a protective embrace the once proud and imperious woman who has become a vulnerable girl.

4.4 ASIDES

The convention of the aside, which involves the audience accepting that the words are unheard by anyone else on stage, would not normally merit isolation as a significant aspect of a dramatist's technique, but in *The Changeling* it has a major function. The aside, like the soliloquy, gives the audience direct access to the thoughts, and therefore to the real nature, of a character. It is very useful in a play about deceptive appearances, because it can highlight for the audience differences between what characters say and what they think. *The Changeling* is very much concerned with the inner nature and the number of asides it contains is very high compared with many other plays of the period. In particular, asides occur frequently and significantly in the two great scenes between Beatrice and De Flores – Act II, scene ii, and Act III, scene iv. They draw attention to the fact that the two characters do not understand each other and are thinking on different lines; Beatrice thinks she will rid herself of both Alonzo and De Flores, whilst the latter anticipates Beatrice being in his power and yielding to him. The asides provide the audience with a strong sense of the danger for the unwitting Beatrice and help to build up suspense and anticipation of the moment when she will discover what she has done. The presence of a significant number of asides emphasises in a literal way that the two people are not communicating. It also indicates that the interest of the dramatists is very much in the 'psychology' of the characters. In Act II, scene ii and Act III, scene iv, the asides show the separation of Beatrice and De Flores, but it is noticeable that when the sexual relationship has been established, and Beatrice relies on him to help to preserve her reputation (V, i) there are no more asides between them. In fact, Beatrice's cunning persuasion of her father to reward De Flores, and the final soliloquy, emphasise strongly that they are now in collusion, keeping their real thoughts and feelings hidden from other people rather than from each other.

4.5 DOUBLE PLOT

The double plot in *The Changeling* is a major means by which the main themes and ideas are expressed and developed. There is a sequential justa-positioning of scenes from the two plots through which contrasts, parallels and connections are set up. The major contrast is that of tone, since the sub-plot set in the madhouse is comic whilst the main plot is tragic, and the development of the former is towards an ending in which faults and foolishness are acknowledged, with improvement in the lives of the characters, whilst the development of the main plot is towards suffering and death. The sub-plot presents the triumph of virtue whilst the main plot shows the overthrow of vice.

Contrasts and connections can be made in terms of characters, situations and themes. Beatrice and Isabella are contrasted as women who are tempted to demand his 'share' (III, iii, 252), and in IV, scene iii, warns Isabella that De Flores and Lollio. De Flores watches the secret meeting of Alsemero and Beatrice and realises this may provide him with the means of achieving his desires (II, ii, 58-60). Lollio overhears Antonio wooing Isabella, tries to demand his 'share' (III, iii, 252), and in IV, scene iii, warns Isabella that if she falls he will claim his 'thirds' (IV, iii, 36-7). The reactions of the two women to these threats are different. Beatrice transgresses and has to submit to blackmail, whilst Isabella threatens to persuade Antonio to cut Lollio's throat. The sub-plot therefore presents an inversion of the main plot. Isabella's ability to resist temptation is made the more striking for the audience because the dramatists take a stock comic situation which is frequently used in the drama of the period, that of the young wife married to an old, foolish and jealous husband, whose cuckolding usually provides opportunity for comic situations. Isabella's fidelity to Alibius despite temptations is therefore the more remarkable. What is even more striking is that this stock comic situation of the young wife outwitting the jealous husband occurs in the tragic main plot with the virginity test. A parallel is suggested between Alsemero and the doctor Alibius through the discovery of his medical and scientific equipment, and the experiments he has marked in his book which suggest that he is concerned about sexual fidelity. This reversal of comic and tragic which subverts audience expectations is the dramatists' means of emphasising their central ideas about sin and temptation.

The themes of the play are developed by the parallel nature of the two plots. A number of critics have noted that the sub-plot expresses in literal form what in the main plot is metaphorical. This is so with regard to the theme of madness. The theme of deceptive appearance which, in the main plot, is concerned with the hiding of a person's real nature finds expression in the sub-plot literally in the disguises of Antonio and Franciscus as fool and madman, and of Isabella as madwoman. The theme of sight and blindness, linked with concerns about deceptive appearance and madness finds expression in the sub-plot particularly at the point where disguises are revealed, with Isabella's scornful words to Antonio, 'You, a quick-sighted lover?' (IV, iii, 137). The main plot's concern with honour is reflected in a section of dialogue between Antonio and Lollio about the nature of honour (IV, iii, 92-103). The main plot references to the Fall of Man find echoes in the sub-plot (III, iii, 181-3; IV, iii, 40-1). To see fully how the main and sub-plots interact in the articulation of themes it is necessary to look at the way in which scenes are juxtaposed so that the concerns of one are echoed or contrasted in what precedes or follows it. A detailed consideration of individual points of connection is given in the Commentary in Section 2 and you should reread that when considering fully the relation of the two plots.

5 SPECIMEN CRITICAL

ANALYSIS

Act II, scene ii, 54–91

BEATRICE	Perfect your service, and conduct this gentleman
	The private way you brought him.
DIAPHANTA	I shall madam. 55
ALSEMERO	My love's as firm as love e'er built upon.

Exeunt DIAPHANTA and ALSEMERO
Enter DE FLORES

DE FLORES	(*aside*) I have watch'd this meeting, and do wonder much
	What shall become of t'other; I'm sure both
	Cannot be serv'd unless she transgress; happily
	Then I'll put in for one; for if a woman 60
	Fly from one point, from him she makes a husband,
	She spreads and mounts then like arithmetic,
	One, ten, a hundred, a thousand, ten thousand,
	Proves in time sutler to an army royal.
	Now I do look to be most richly rail'd at, 65
	Yet I must see her.
BEATRICE	(*aside*) Why put case I loath'd him
	As much as youth and beauty hates a sepulchre,
	Must I needs show it? Cannot I keep that secret,
	And serve my turn upon him? – See, he's here.
	– De Flores!
DE FLORES	(*aside*) Ha, I shall run mad with joy! 70
	She call'd me fairly by my name, De Flores,
	And neither rogue nor rascal.
BEATRICE	What ha' you done
	To your face a-late? Y'have met with some good physician;
	Y'have prun'd yourself, methinks; you were not wont
	To look so amorously.
DE FLORES	(*aside*) Not I; 75
	'Tis the same physnomy, to a hair and pimple,
	Which she call'd scurvy scarce an hour ago;
	How is this?

BEATRICE	Come hither; nearer, man.	
DE FLORES	(*aside*) I'm up to the chin in heaven!	
BEATRICE	Turn, let me see;	

BEATRICE   Turn, let me see;
Faugh, 'tis but the heat of the liver, I perceiv't;   80
I thought it had been worse.

DE FLORES   (*aside*)   Her fingers touch'd me!
She smells all amber.

BEATRICE   I'll make a water for you shall cleanse this
Within a fortnight.

DE FLORES   With your own hands, lady?

BEATRICE   Yes, mine own, sir; in a work of cure   85
I'll trust no other.

DE FLORES   (*aside*)   'Tis half an act of pleasure
To hear her talk thus to me.

BEATRICE   When w'are us'd
To a hard face, 'tis not so unpleasing;
It mends still in opinion, hourly mends,
I see it by experience.

DE FLORES   (*aside*)   I was blest   90
To light upon this minute; I'll make use on't.

The secret meeting of Beatrice and Alsemero draws to a close as she instructs her waiting-woman to conduct him back to his room. Beatrice's words at the opening of the extract prefigure ironically what is to happen between Alsemero and Diaphanta later on the wedding-night. The secretness of the meeting is underlined by the reference to 'The private way'. A conscious attempt is being made to ensure that other people do not see or know about it. The style of Beatrice and Alsemero's lines is self-consciously poetic and elevated, as they create for themselves a sense of this being a meeting of honourable lovers beset by dangers rather than a clandestine meeting of a betrothed woman and the man she wishes to be her lover. Beatrice's words to Diaphanta suggest that she is acting the role of princess or high-born lady in an heroic love tale. The style reminds us of her words to Jasperino at the beginning of the previous scene when he came to arrange the meeting – 'Good angels and this conduct be your guide' (II, i, 3). The irony of all this is evident here because the audience know that Beatrice has just had the idea of using De Flores to rid herself of Alonzo and has used the term 'blood-guiltiness', which suggests a contrast to the noble and virtuous woman she wishes Alsemero to think she is. He replies with an affirmation of the strength of his love in similar terms. The image of the building securely constructed is perhaps intended to remind us of Vermandero's castle which develops into an image of central significance in the play. Middleton skilfully makes the audience aware of the discrepancy between the image which Beatrice wishes to project for Alsemero and the reality of her desire and intentions by giving her words and phrases which carry the possibility of double meanings. Although she intends to sound like a noble lady and to be talking of honourable actions, 'Perfect your service', 'The private way' and 'serve my turn upon him' have a possible level of sexual reference which would not have been lost on the Jacobean audience.

The appearance of De Flores is unexpected and shocks the audience. He has not been in view during the meeting but his first words indicate that he has watched all. Had the dramatists had him present throughout the first part of the scene to make this point, audience attention would have been distracted from sole concentration on the relationship of Beatrice and Alsemero. An effect of shock is also created by the sudden change in style from Alsemero's high-sounding love sentiments to the directness and cynicism of De Flores's speech. If the dramatists had given hints of sexual meaning in Beatrice's words, for instance, 'Perfect your service', De Flores's use of the term, 'I'm sure both/Cannot be serv'd unless she transgress', more clearly has baser and explicitly sexual suggestions, linked to the idea of transgression, and emphasised by the use of the word 'mounts'. The dramatists may be suggesting that whereas Beatrice will not admit her sexual desire for Alsemero, De Flores is quite open about his interest in her. The play upon the word 'service' is a feature of the scene as it later develops.

There is a quality of mocking humour in De Flores's speech which presents a tonal contrast to those of Beatrice and Alsemero. The mocking humour is achieved through the use of an incongruous image and exaggeration. The woman who gains a taste for sin is likened to an arithmetical calculation in which the sum grows larger and larger. He sees her as becoming increasingly promiscuous until, in a final gesture of imaginative hyperbole, he suggests that she will become the supplier of sex to a whole army.

Humorous effect continues in the latter part of this extract through De Flores's surprise at Beatrice's reaction to him. He expects to be greeted with anger and abuse and prepares himself for it, but he is then taken by surprise at her kind greeting. It is amusing to see the man who has just been pleased to have discovered a secret and who has been calculating his chances suddenly taken off-guard by the unexpected. He still retains a grip on reality, noting the inherently ludicrous nature of the situation in which Beatrice praises his face which is exactly the same as 'she call'd scurvy scarce an hour' before. He cannot understand what has caused this change, and momentarily at least he is taken in by it as Beatrice tells him to come close to her and then touches him. She uses physical proximity and contact to work on him, and with some success as his asides express an intensity of sensuous response, mentioning her touch and her perfume, and going on to suggest that her gentle words alone give him a quasi-sexual experience: ''Tis half an act of pleasure/To hear her talk thus to me.'

The use of the aside is very marked in this extract. At this moment Beatrice and De Flores are not talking directly to each other, and through the asides in this scene the audience have a strong sense of the discrepancy between appearance and reality. Beatrice talks of dissembling her loathing for De Flores in terms of keeping a secret, a word which recurs frequently in the play. She compares him with a 'sepulchre' or tomb, and the association with death is apt; he will not only become her agent of death by murdering Alonzo, but will also bring her to destruction. She is playing with danger and the speech underlines her recklessness. Her self-centred use of other people is clearly indicated by her words 'And serve my turn upon him'. The irony is that he will serve his turn sexually upon her. There is also dramatic irony in Beatrice's lines about De Flores's face. Pretending, she says that his disfigurement is not as bad as she had thought and that his face is not so unpleasing once one is accustomed to it. Here she does not mean what she says, but later in the play she does come to love what she now loathes. The imagery of sickness and of curing is also ironic in that by her actions she will destroy her own moral health. This imagery reminds us of the doctor, Alibius, who attempts to cure the madmen in his asylum.

At the end of the extract De Flores begins to regain his control of the situation and thinks how he might use it to his advantage, though he does not yet realise the insincerity of Beatrice's affectionate attitude towards him. The scene is full of danger signals, and this extract comes at the moment when Beatrice will take a decisive and fatal step. It is a turning-point of the play.

6 CRITICAL RECEPTION AND APPROACHES

In its own time *The Changeling* appears to have been popular, and references to the play in the first half of the seventeenth century suggest that its success arose from the sub-plot and the character of Antonio, not, as in our own time, from the scenes of psychological realism between Beatrice and De Flores. The fact that the play was first published during the period of the Commonwealth (1649-60) when the theatres were closed, and that it was performed several times in the early years of the Restoration period (after Charles II had been restored as king in 1660) when they were re-opened, indicates the standing it had and the popularity it enjoyed in the seventeenth century. Samuel Pepys recorded a visit to a successful performance at the Salisbury Court Theatre on 23 February 1660 or 1661.

In the eighteenth and nineteenth centuries the play does not appear to have been performed, but since the 1930s it has received increasing critical and theatrical interest. It is now regarded as one of the major plays of the Jacobean period; one critic, T. B. Tomlinson, even goes so far as to say '*The Changeling* is, outside Shakespeare, the most obviously intelligent play in English' (*A Study of Elizabethan and Jacobean Tragedy*, p. 186). The interest is evident both in the increasing number of books on Thomas Middleton and the number of productions which his plays now receive. In 1978-9 there were no fewer than four professional productions of *The Changeling*, two of which were in London, one at the Riverside Studios directed by Peter Gill, and the other by Terry Hands for the Royal Shakespeare Company. In November 1985 it was possible within a fortnight to see three different Middleton plays, including *The Changeling*, performed at the Bear Gardens Theatre Museum in Southwark by professional companies.

The main interest of twentieth-century critics of *The Changeling* has been in the psychological exploration of the Beatrice-De Flores relationship. In 1936, in her book, *The Jacobean Drama*, Una Ellis-Fermor compared Middleton with the nineteenth-century writer Henrik Ibsen in his observation of human psychology, and this comparison was taken up again by T. B. Tomlinson in 1964. Critics have been divided over the interest and artistic integrity of the sub-plot. William Empson and M. C. Bradbrook in particular argued for a close thematic relation between main plot and sub-plot, and although there have been a few dissenting voices, most recent works, such as Nicholas Brooke's *Horrid Laughter in Jacobean Tragedy* accept that the sub-plot is an integral part of the play's design.

In the 1960s *The Changeling* was approached by critics such as Robert Ornstein and Irving Ribner from the point of view of its moral values. In recent years important studies, such as Dorothy Farr's *Thomas Middleton and the Drama of Realism*, have drawn attention to the connections between Middleton's comedies and tragedies, and have enhanced understanding of the comic and tragic elements in *The Changeling*. Current critical approaches focus upon the play in relation to the social, political and religious concerns of the times in which it was written, as in Margot Heinemann's, *Puritanism and Theatre*, or on the text of the play in relation to performance, as in Michael Scott's lively book, *Renaissance Drama and a Modern Audience*.

REVISION QUESTIONS

The purpose of these questions is to help you to develop your understanding of the play more fully by exploring important aspects in depth. They may provide a focus for your own private study, or a basis for discussion with others, or you might use them for written answers. Writing an answer will make you sort out and develop your ideas and will sometimes make you realise that points which you thought you had understood have not been fully grasped.

1. To what extent would it be true to say that there is no character in the play who is admirable or even likeable, or for whom we feel pity, and to what extent does that matter?
2. 'Beatrice is not a moral creature; she becomes moral only by becoming damned.' Do you agree? Consider to what extent Beatrice has a sense of guilt.
3. Alsemero has been described as 'the equal and opposite of De Flores', equal in his reasoning powers and his sexual attraction and opposite in his morality. In what ways does your study of the character lead you to agree or disagree with this?
4. 'De Flores elicits from the audience a variety of responses, fascination, amusement, pity, horror, repulsion.' Consider where in the play, and for what reasons, we respond in a variety of ways to him, and whether you feel the list of responses given here is complete and accurate.
5. To what extent would it be accurate or adequate to describe De Flores as the villain of the play?
6. 'Upon yon meteor ever hung my fate.' This line about De Flores might suggest that Beatrice's downfall was inevitable from the beginning. Do you consider that to be the case, and how does that affect the play's tragic impact?
7. Would you agree that the multiple deceptions of the play all arise in the first place from self-deception?

8. 'A victim of her society as well as herself.' How important to the tragedy are social matters such as social regulations, propriety and status? Do you agree that Beatrice is a victim of her society?

9. 'The society of the play is one in which people are isolated in their self-centredness; their blindness, their foolishness, and their miscalculations all arise from this fact.' Discuss this statement and consider in what different ways self-centredness and isolation are shown in the play.

10. Examine the ways in which connections are made between love and madness in the play, and consider what view or views of love are conveyed by these connections.

11. Though love seems to be a major concern, to what extent might *The Changeling* be said to be more about the emotions of lust and fear?

12. To what extent is it possible to separate comic and tragic elements in the play?

13. Consider the varied ways in which irony is used in the play and the dramatic effects created by it.

14. Examine the ways in which the theme of 'secrets' is presented and developed.

15. What different types of contrast and reversal are to be found in *The Changeling*, and what is conveyed through the use of these dramatic techniques?

FURTHER READING

The introductions to the following editions of *The Changeling* are recommended:
  The Revels edition, ed. N. W. Bawcutt (Methuen, 1958).
  The New Mermaid edition, ed. Patrician Thomson (Ernest Benn, 1964).

Selected critical works

Barker, Richard Hindry, *Thomas Middleton* (Columbia University Press, 1958) pp. 121-31.
Bradbrook, M. C., *Themes and Conventions of Elizabethan Tragedy* (Cambridge University Press, 1935; reprinted, 1969) pp. 213-24 (in reprint).
Brooke, Nicholas, *Horrid Laughter in Jacobean Tragedy* (Open Books, 1979), pp. 70-88.
Ellis-Fermor, Una, *The Jacobean Drama* (Methuen, 1936; reprinted 1969) pp. 144-52 (in reprint).
Empson, William, *Some Versions of Pastoral* (Chatto & Windus, 1935; Penguin Books, 1966) pp. 45-8 (in reprint).
Farr, Dorothy, *Thomas Middleton and the Drama of Realism* (Oliver & Boyd, 1973) pp. 50-71.
Heinemann, Margot, *Puritanism and Theatre* (Cambridge University Press, 1980) pp. 172-99.
Levin, Richard, *The Multiple Plot in English Renaissance Drama* (University of Chicago Press, 1971) pp. 38-48.
Ornstein, Robert, *The Moral Vision of Jacobean Tragedy* (University of Wisconsin Press, 1960; reprinted by Greenwood Press, 1975) pp. 179-90 (in reprint).
Ribner, Irving, *Jacobean Tragedy* (Methuen, 1962; reprinted, 1979) pp. 123-37 (in reprint).
Schoenbaum, Samuel, *Middleton's Tragedies* (Columbia University Press, 1955) pp. 130-52 (in reprint).
Scott, Michael, *Renaissance Drama and a Modern Audience* (Macmillan, 1982) pp. 76-88.
Tomlinson, T. B., *A Study of Elizabethan and Jacobean Tragedy* (Cambridge University Press, 1964) pp. 184-212.